*T*HE volumes of the University of Michigan Studies and Publications are published by authority of the Board of Regents under the direction of the Executive Board of the Graduate School. The contributors are chiefly, but not exclusively, members of the faculties or graduates of the University. The expense is borne in part by gifts, in part by appropriations of the Board of Regents. A list of volumes already published or in preparation is given at the end of this volume. The other volumes in this series are listed on pages vi-vii.

University of Michigan Publications

LANGUAGE AND LITERATURE

VOLUME XI

FRENCH MODAL SYNTAX IN THE SIXTEENTH CENTURY

FRENCH MODAL SYNTAX
IN THE
SIXTEENTH CENTURY

BY

NEWTON S. BEMENT

THE UNIVERSITY OF MICHIGAN

ANN ARBOR

UNIVERSITY OF MICHIGAN PRESS

1934

PREFACE

THE mechanical aspects of French modal syntax were somewhat obscured in the sixteenth century by the diversity of structural accidents attending subordination and by the imperfect differentiation of moods—of the present subjunctive, for example, from the future indicative, of the imperfect subjunctive from the present conditional, of the imperative from the present subjunctive. This fact led me to consider, at the outset, the possible effect of style on modal syntax, but I was unable to discern any very appreciable one, except in the styles employed in pleading and in orders emanating from final authority. The conscious choice of mood as a stylistic ornament appears to be a seventeenth-century innovation. Modal syntax that Maupas or Vaugelas might have defined as elegant in the seventeenth century was quite accidental in the sixteenth. French modal syntax in the sixteenth century seems merely to follow the natural growth of the language, submitting at one point to the influence of mechanical analogy and at another stubbornly resisting dissimulation in the presence of structural differentia, but maintaining withal a certain logical unity.

For the purpose of determining the general facts or rules of this syntax as it is exemplified in the language of representative writers from Commynes to Malherbe, and for the further purpose of discerning the changes or developments which occur in it during that period, I have employed the method customarily used in comparative studies: mechanization of the language. The procedure in this instance consisted in the definition of verb forms or definition of eligible material, the examination of the circumstances of subjunctive usage, the examination of mood usage in all examples syntactically related to examples of subjunctive usage, and, finally, the organization of results in a manner to permit the greatest brevity in their presentation as well as the greatest pre-

v

cision in their formulation. Subsequently, for the purpose of comparison, the study was extended beyond the limits of the period defined. Its present form might be described as a contribution to a comparative grammar of French modal syntax in the sixteenth century.

The obvious function of such a grammar would be to fill a lacuna in the history of the French language, possibly in the manner anticipated by M. Brunot where, in his *Histoire de la langue française des origines à 1900* (I, xxi), he envisages "une série de travaux qui complètent mes indications."

"La syntaxe des modes," says M. Brunot (*op. cit.*, II, 444), with reference to the sixteenth century, "ne paraît pas s'être beaucoup éclaircie ni fixée. C'est à peine si dans un ou deux ordres de propositions, l'usage marque des tendances un peu claires." This conclusion is presumably different from the one which Darmesteter and Hatzfeld might have expected, if one may judge from the comments in their work *Le Seizième Siècle en France* (p. 268):

"L'usage du subjonctif dans les propositions subordonnées, tel qu'il est fixé dans la langue actuelle, ne concorde plus entièrement avec celui que connaissait le seizième siècle et qui rappelle la tradition du moyen âge. Nous ne pouvons qu'indiquer ce point qui . . . mériterait une étude spéciale, et prêterait matière à de longs développements."

The lacuna invites, as Darmesteter and Hatzfeld imply, a specialized study on a broad and comparative basis, both for the purpose of discerning transitions in modal syntax and in order to formulate the body of rules which governed it during the sixteenth century.

In attempting to fill this lacuna I realize that the subject cannot be exhausted by an individual and that each addition to it must be, like the present increment, partly cumulative, partly confirmative, and partly corrective. I have sought, nevertheless, through the dispositions governing the selection and interpretation of material, to insure the results so far as possible against error.

The form in which the results are presented, besides bearing witness to the regularity of the language of the period, is intended to render them instantly accessible for study or comparison.

I take this opportunity to thank Dr. Arthur G. Canfield of the University of Michigan for his generous encouragement and counsel, and to express my indebtedness to Dr. John R. Reinhard, also of the University of Michigan, for his very helpful reading of the manuscript.

N. S. B.

CONTENTS

Contents

Contents

FRENCH MODAL SYNTAX IN THE
SIXTEENTH CENTURY

ABBRÉVIATIONS

A.	Les Amours	Gaut.	Gautier d'Arras
Amy.	Jacques Amyot	Malh.	François de Malherbe
Brun.	Ferdinand Brunot	Marg.	Marguerite d'Angoulême
Calv.	Jean Calvin	Maup.	Charles Maupas
Chass.	A. Chassang	Mont.	Michel de Montaigne
Chr.	Chrétien de Troyes	O. F.	Œuvres françoises
Comm.	Philippe de Commynes	Oud.	Antoine Oudin
Desp.	Bonaventure des Périers	P.	Pantagruel
Est.	Henri Estienne	P. R.	Propos rustiques
Eutr.	Contes et discours	Paliss.	Bernard Palissy
	d'Eutrapel	R. C.	Institution de la religion
Fail	Noël du Fail		chrestienne
Fr.	La Franciade	Rab.	François Rabelais
France	Anatole France	Rons.	Pierre de Ronsard
Froiss.	Jean Froissart	Vair	Guillaume du Vair
G.	Gargantua	Vaug.	Claude Favre de Vaugelas

INTRODUCTION

THE works selected for examination in this study of French modal syntax in the sixteenth century include two by writers who apparently knew no Latin, Commynes and Palissy; one which was originally composed in Latin, Calvin's *Institution de la religion chrestienne;* and one by a writer who spoke Latin primarily, Montaigne. They also include a work based on a Greek original, by Amyot, one on the French language itself, by Henri Estienne, one by a royal linguist, Marguerite d'Angoulême, and one by her scholarly attendant, Des Périers. Malherbe's letters add to this list the informal compositions of a reputedly meticulous practician. Among the authors of the other works selected are a representative of the medical profession, Rabelais, a representative of the legal profession, Du Fail, a poet, Ronsard, and an orator, Du Vair. Such are the results of the dispositions taken in regard to the chronological spacing and the linguistic, social, and geographical range of material to be examined.

Frequency tables employed to determine what amount of material must be examined in order to ascertain a writer's predominant usages revealed that two hundred pages, and in some instances one hundred and fifty, were sufficient.[1] On completion of the study, however, when the superior linguistic range of Calvin's work had become evident, it seemed advisable to complete the examination of the monumental *Institution* and to present the result, along with an additional list of expressions and constructions, in an appendix.

The definition of eligible examples of usage in the material thus selected and delimited rests upon a comparative examination of their verb forms and those employed by contemporary grammarians.

---

[1] In actual practice it was deemed best to employ a greater amount ordinarily. The pagination may be consulted in the Bibliography of Authors, p. 164. This pagination indicates minimum rather than maximum limits, since in practice it appears impossible to confine linguistic research to a set number of pages.

I

The grammarians of the sixteenth century do not achieve a standard, correct, or commonly recognized set of conjugations or paradigms, despite their evident progress towards the correct division set up by Oudin in 1640.[2] Variations in the personal endings of verbal forms, however, rarely occur within the limits of a given grammar, and the different grammars, moreover, are essentially in agreement on this point. They are also somewhat in advance of contemporary literature, in regard to the regular and positive distinction of mood through verbal forms, while in mood usage they are somewhat behind it.

The results of the comparative examination showed that to follow closely a given dictum or standard, in determining mood through form, would be constantly to risk falling into error. Standards which appear to be applicable at the end of the sixteenth century would be extremely misleading if applied to material composed at the beginning of the century or even at the middle. Malherbe, for example, is astonished to find an indicative *eust* in the poetry of Desportes, and his astonishment proceeds apparently from a belief that Desportes has employed the subjunctive mood (Malh., IV, 398). Darmesteter (*Cours*, 4ᵉ partie, 125) regards the indeterminate form *continuez* as an indicative form in *je desire que vous continuez* (Mont., II, 608).

Generally speaking, in the period from Commynes to Malherbe the terminations *-ons* and *-ez* of the present tense are indeterminate, and the terminations *-ions* and *-iez* are subjunctive. In the past definite or simple tense and in the imperfect subjunctive the terminations of the third singular form are indeterminate, except that, ordinarily but not invariably, the termination *-a* is indicative and the terminations *-at* and *-ast* are subjunctive. It is impossible, however, to provide a constantly reliable set of criteria for distinguishing mood through form. The work of each writer requires separate study, for the purpose of cataloguing doubtful forms.

In order to preclude the possibility of errors all doubtful forms, however well founded one's opinion concerning the intention of the

---

[2] The Bibliography may be consulted on pages 161-168 and a list of abbreviations on page xviii.

writer might be, were relegated into the indeterminate class. It is under this heading that their occurrences are registered in the Index of Expressions and Constructions. In the text indeterminate forms are indicated by asterisks.

The occasional inclusion, in the text, of examples drawn from the works of two twelfth-century writers, one fourteenth-century writer, and one modern writer, and their representation in the Index, are the result of extending the comparative phase of the study.

The titles of my previous publications in this field [3] indicate indirectly the limits of the present publication, but the Index of Expressions and Constructions, though incomplete in the lexical sense, is not correspondingly restricted (see p. 127).

These titles explain, for example, the absence of a chapter on adverbial clauses of condition, a subject pertaining to the history of the conditional sentence during this period. The history of the conditional sentence is mainly that of rise or decline in the employment of various combinations of tenses and moods, some of which constitute constructional formulas so persistent that they control the modal syntax of objective and relative clauses incorporated in the conditional sentence.

In addition to serving in the conditional sentence as the secondary form of an apodosis or a protasis, the relative or adjectival clause serves also as the secondary form of other types of clauses, and its modality is identical with that of the corresponding objective or consecutive clause. The effect of negation, interrogation, and condition on modality is likewise essentially the same in adjectival clauses as in objective clauses, since the primary tend-

[3]"Petrus Ramus and the Beginnings of Formal French Grammar," *Romanic Review*, XIX (1928), 309-323; "The Subjunctive in Relative Clauses from Commynes to Malherbe," *Philological Quarterly*, X (1931), 294-306; "The Conditional Sentence from Commynes to Malherbe," *Romanic Review, Supplement* (1931), or *Publications of the Institute of French Studies, Inc.* (Columbia University), 26 p.; "The French Imperfect Subjunctive and Present Conditional in the Sixteenth Century," *PMLA*, XLVII (1932), 992-1011; "Some Phonological, Orthographical, and Syntactical Aspects of the Persistence of the French Present Subjunctive Endings *-ONS* and *-EZ*" [The historical relationship between the eventual orthographical representation of the yod in these endings, the apparently syntactical origin of the plural imperative forms, and the use of optative *que*], *Papers of the Michigan Academy of Science, Arts and Letters*, XVIII (1932), 505-524.

ency of the modality of the adjectival clause is to conform to the nature of the antecedent. The nature of the antecedent requires historical definition, however, in those instances in which the apparent antecedent is superlative in form.

A separate comparative study and summary of the usage of the imperfect subjunctive and present conditional has also been made, for the purpose of examining the process of their differentiation. It is necessarily more concerned than the present study with the historical significance of moods and with tenses and tense sequence, especially since, for example, the use of the present subjunctive replacing the imperfect, after the present conditional, appears to have been a consequence of this differentiation.

In the sixteenth century there was still some tendency to retain the imperative forms in hypotaxis, but the delay in distinguishing the corresponding subjunctive forms orthographically from the modern plural imperative forms seems to be mainly attributable to the analogical influence of verbs having a yod in the stem. Although this matter forms a vital part of the history of French modal syntax, I have permitted it to have but little bearing on the present study except with reference to the isolation of indeterminate forms.

The organization of the study, based upon the grammatical division reflected by the chapter headings and subheadings, is clarified so far as possible by means of the form given to the table of contents, which is intended for consultation as an outline introduction to the text.

CHAPTER I

AFTER DECLARATIVE EXPRESSIONS

IN OBJECTIVE CLAUSES

After Affirmative Verbs

1. After verbs expressing certainty (type: *savoir, connaître*) the subjunctive is very exceptional:

Toutesfoys ne laissa pas la mere d'y regarder, & quant se vint à dire Ite missa est *congneut* veritablement que iamais deux freres d'une ventrée ne *fussent* si semblables. (Marg., III, 89)

In this example *fussent* appears to have pluperfect force and to be employed with the sense of a conditional of conjecture. Such an employment of a past tense of the subjunctive is not rare (e.g., Malh., III, 114; Desp., 48).

2. Among verbs of the suppositive type subjunctive usage was observed after the following ones:

croire	pouvoir estimer
faire croire	trouver vraisemblable
cuider	se douter
penser	conjecturer
pouvoir penser	soupçonner
estimer	

Je *croy* qu'elle n'y *soit* plus maintenant. (Rab., G., 21-7); donne moy quelque raison . . . pour me *faire croyre* que ton dire *soit* fondé sur quelque preuve legitime. (Paliss., 165); on *cuyde* que ce ne *soit* qu'une fable (Desp., 347); je *pense* que ce *soit* quelque ouvrage de barbares. (Malh., III, 330); Mais bien ay je ouy dire que on ne sçait où il est, & *estime* lon quil *soit* pendu. (Fail, P. R., 96); je *trouve vray-semblable* qu'il *aye* regardé plus avant (Mont., I, 98); je *me doubte* que la playe *soit* vieille. (Rab., P., 15-89); par les grands biens dont ilz jouissent, nous *conjecturons* qu'ilz *soyent* immortelz (Amy., 14); *soupsonnant* que quelques uns *fussent* cachez là dedans (Marg., I, 154).

5

Songer is little used as yet. Later, Vaugelas approves its use for *penser*. No example of subjunctive usage was noted after it. Chrétien de Troyes throws some light on its sense:

> Mes tot aussi con cil qui *songe*,
> Qui por verité croit mançonge,
> Les *feisoient* li escu *croire*,
> Que ceste mançonge *fust* voire.
> (Chr., 2103)

Faire croire, Vaugelas says, implies truth, and *faire accroire*, falsity (Vaug.-Chass., I, 402). This is true for *faire accroire*, both during our period[1] and earlier, but mood usage after it is predominantly indicative, and the subjunctive occurs more frequently after *faire croire*, although one would expect the reverse to be true. The subjunctive is employed, in fact, after expressions signifying "to believe mistakenly," as may be determined from the context of examples like the following:

il *croit* que . . . je la vous *aye* communiquée (Malh., III, 87); ilz *cuidoyent* que ce *fussent* hommes qui . . . (Amy., 76); *pensant* que ie *fusse* une pauvre meschante. (Marg., I, 82); il *estimoit* qu'il *allast* espiant le poinct de son occasion (Amy., 72).

But the indicative occurs in similar circumstances:

Je *croy* que c'*est* là une corne de limasson (Rab., G., 38-23); elle *pensoit* que sa fille *estoit* morte (Marg., II, 70).

The truth is that believing mistakenly or believing correctly does not affect mood usage, and that mood usage is indifferent:

ilz *cuidoyent* que ce (mistakenly) *fussent* hommes qui (correctly) *courussent* ainsi ça et là (Amy., 76); la meilleure partie des nostres *pense* (mistakenly) que la Franciade *soit* une histoire des rois de France (Rons., Fr., 8); ils *pensoyent* (mistakenly) que le vray fils d'Hector *estoit* mort (*id.*, Fr., 12); j'*estime* qu'il n'*avoit* pas escrit Ouan, ains que ce *soit* une faute de l'impression. (Est., 172); un intendant . . . le pria de lui dire en ami s'il *croyoit* que nous *eussions* guerre, et si 58 reviendroit (Malh., III, 398).

To this group of verbs may be added the following, which are even more strongly suppositive, and after which we find the subjunctive:

[1] These words, "our period," designate the period from Commynes to Malherbe, inclusive, wherever they are employed. See the Preface.

présupposer (Est., 5)   prendre le cas (Desp., 199)
poser (Vair, 75)   feindre (Vair, 181)
poser le cas (Paliss., 163)

It is rather peculiar that after *supposer* the indicative is already predominant in Froissart's work.

We may say that mood usage has no connection with the correctness or incorrectness of the opinion or belief expressed and that the theory that such a connection exists is fallacious. After affirmative verbs of the suppositive type usage is erratic, but it is slowly changing in favor of the indicative. The following table[2] shows the percentages of subjunctive usage in the several works examined:

Gaut.	69	Desp.	10	Est.	22
Chr.	75	Calv.	11	Mont.	23
Froiss.	58	Fail	15	Vair	2
Comm.	20	Rons.	11	Malh.	6
Marg.	10	Paliss.	14	France	0
Rab.	25	Amy.	20		

Let us examine also the mood frequency tables of the representative verbs *cuider, croire,* and *penser:*

Key to columns: number of occurrences followed by (1) indicative; (2) future; (3) conditional; (4) indeterminate verb form; (5) subjunctive; (6) subjunctive employed with conditional force.

cuider	(1)	(2)	(3)	(4)	(5)	(6)
Gaut.	2	—	—	2	16	—
Chr.	3	—	2	1	14	—
Froiss.	—	—	—	—	13	—
Comm.	—	—	—	13	9	—
Marg.	—	—	—	11	3	1
Rab.	—	—	—	—	1	—
Desp.	—	—	—	4	1	—
Calv. O. F.	—	—	—	—	1	—
Fail	—	—	—	—	1	—
Paliss.	1	—	—	—	1	1
Amy.	—	—	—	1	2	2

[2] In tables the names of authors are given in chronological order. Since occurrences were counted only by myself, I do not assume that frequency tables are infallible.

croire	(1)	(2)	(3)	(4)	(5)	(6)
Gaut.	—	2	—	—	—	—
Chr.	—	—	—	—	4	—
Froiss.	5	4	3	1	1	—
Comm.	27	1	1	11	—	15c[3]
Marg.	52	8	8	16	1	7
Rab.	10	2c	—	6	2	—
Desp.	24	1	1	4	1	1
Calv. R. C.	5	—	—	—	—	—
Fail	10	2	3	1	1	—
Rons.	2	1	—	—	—	—
Paliss.	14	1	1	4	1	—
Amy.	3	—	—	—	—	—
Est.	2	3	1	2	—	—
Mont.	4	—	1	1	—	—
Vair	12	3	5	4	—	—
Malh.	35	37	4	14	2	—
France	14	—	2	—	—	—
penser						
Gaut.	3	1	1	2	—	—
Chr.	2	1	—	1	1	—
Froiss.	1	—	2	—	—	—
Comm.	5	—	2	2	2	—
Marg.	47	2	21	44	9	—
Rab.	10	—	—	17	4	—
Desp.	19	2	2	23	3	1
Calv. R. C.	6	2	—	1	1	—
Fail	3	—	1	2	1	1
Rons.	3	—	2	1	1	—
Paliss.	8	—	3	1	2	—
Amy.	2	—	4	4	2	—
Est.	1	1	—	1	2	—
Mont.	1	—	—	1	—	—
Vair	12	5	5	3	1	1
Malh.	10	3	4	—	1	—
France	11	—	2	—	—	—

These verbs were apparently synonyms:

> Li dus, qui *cuide* et *croit* et *panse*
> Que Cligés n'et vers lui deffanse
> (Chr., 4011)

[3] The addition of the letter *c* to the number of occurrences indicates that they were found in conditional sentences.

The tables show, in sum, *cuider* being displaced by *croire*, the subjunctive persisting after *cuider*, and, after *croire* and *penser*, the indicative predominant and becoming more so in proportion as *cuider* is dropped from usage.

3. After verbs of the assertive type the indicative is predominant, but the subjunctive is not extremely exceptional. Subjunctive usage was noted after:

dire	corner (Rab., G., 5-101)
vouloir dire (Mont., I, 98)	se glorifier (Calv., O. F., 98)

Subjunctive usage in these cases is traceable to: (1) assimilation to the sense of the suppositives or (2) extraneous influence.

(1) Car quant à ceulx qui *disent* que rendre la cause *soit* oster la signifiance du signe, ilz ne considerent pas que . . . (Amy., 10).

(2) Et ce *sera bien à propos* de *dire* qu'elle *dorme* (Calv., O. F., 57); *Quelle folie est-ce* de *dire* . . . que ceux qui . . ., n'y *puissent* rien! (*id.*, O. F., 116); Je ne sçay à quoy il tient qu'il n'en a desja du tout fouldroyé et perdu ce malheureux monde, *de dire* que ces traistres humains non seulement luy *ayent* osé retenir son livre, où est toute sa prescience, mais encores, comme si c'estoit par injure et mocquerie, ilz luy en *ont* envoyé ung au lieu d'icelluy (Desp., 326).

These two groups, it is evident, cannot be sharply distinguished from each other. In the second especially, subjunctive usage appears to be due to some extraneous cause such as emotion, volition, denial, or condition. Or it may be brought about through attraction when the verb *dire* itself is employed subjunctively:

Et *prendray* . . . *à gloire* qu'on *die* de moy que plus en vin *aye* despendu que en huyle (Rab., G., Prol.-83); vous *ne contesterez* que je vous *die* que je *sois* votre serviteur (Malh., III, 576); Je ne suis pas *étonné* qu'elle *die* que l'âme de notre bon roi *soit* au ciel; mais je ne sais comme entendre qu'il fut martyr. (*id.*, III, 222)

In occasional examples of indirect discourse the subjunctive is carried over from an optative employment in direct discourse, and we find it after verbs which may express volition, but which appear to be employed declaratively:

La fille . . . luy *dist* que Dieu *fust*[*4] loué [La fille lui dit: «Dieu soit loué!»] (Marg., I, 122); La Reine *dit* que ceci [la montre des troupes] lui coûtera

[4] The asterisk indicates an indeterminate form. See the Introduction.

un million d'or, et que le peuple *soit* mangé, et puis ce [la guerre] ne sera rien. (Malh., III, 310); possibly *id.*, III, 222, above.

The controlling thought is sometimes merely implied. For example, doubt is implied in a demand for proof:

prouve moy en bonne Logique que bonnet en teste tu *aie* (Fail, Eutr., 213). Compare: Eutrapel . . . vouloit prouver . . que ce n'estoit à un tel galant, et ne luy appartenoit ouvrir . . . de tels . . . propos (*id.*, Eutr., 236).

In studying the language of this period we find, however, both logical usage and erratic usage, frequently side by side. We can only seek to discern, reveal, and summarize the general tendencies.

4. After verbs denoting expectancy (*attendre, s'attendre, espérer*) the future and conditional become predominant. This fact hinges mainly on a tendency which is prevalent far beyond the narrow limits of this particular case, a tendency of the present conditional to displace the imperfect subjunctive in many cases where the latter is still comparatively frequent in the work of Commynes.

Ilz *s'attendoient* qu'on *sonnast* les cloches à leur venue (Comm., II, 38); son medecin . . . à qui chascun moys donnoit dix mil escus, *esperant* qu'il luy *allongeast* la vie. (*id.*, II, 314)

J'*attendois* que selon la coutume, lorsque la Reine seroit partie, ces princesses se *salueroient*, mais elles n'en firent rien. (Malh., III, 477); lon *esperoit* que ce ne *seroit* que lamentations . . ., ce ne fut en verité que consolation (Vair, 22).

5. We find the subjunctive also in attributive dependent clauses after expressions corresponding to those in §2 and §4:

avoir opinion (Est., 146)	être en suspicion (Comm., I, 153)
demeurer en opinion	faire compte (Malh., III, 158)
être d'opinion (Malh., III, 332)	avoir espérance

Quant à Brachmar . . ., je *demeure* bien tousjours *en ceste opinion* qu'il *soit* dict au lieu de Brachmach (Est., 196).

De nostre roy, j'*ay esperance*, comme j'ay dit, que Nostre Seigneur *ayt eu* misericorde de luy et *aura* de tous autres, s'il luy plaist. (Comm., II, 340)

Or the clause may express a predicate:

Dieu veuille que *la première nouvelle* que vous aurez de moi *soit* que Monsieur le légat *ait avancé* quelque chose! (Malh., III, 164)

Construction does not appear to affect mood usage, however, if we except inversion. In cases of inversion the subjunctive is employed ordinarily:

qu'il [Benne] *soit* du vieil François . . ., nous *avons le tesmoignage* de Festus (Est., 176); Rab., G., 28-39; France, 199, 244.

6. The declarative verb is occasionally employed as part of an expression having a special sense which accounts for subjunctive usage:

Il feroit beau voir que nous *eussions fait* un composé pour un crocheteur, . . . et que nous *vousissions* demourer courts (Est., 158) — i.e., On trouverait étrange que . . . .

Il faict beau voir [irony, disapproval] que . . . nostre sapience *apreigne* des bestes mesmes les plus utiles enseignemens (Mont., III, 358).

7. We may hardly assume that all, or even many, of the evolutions observable in the usages of a language are conscious, but we may fairly assume that clarity is sought at all stages of development. The first aid to clarity in the transmission of thought is a uniform practice of some sort, as, for example, the employment of the subjunctive in inversions. Subjunctive usage after declarative expressions, however, is of no value to clarity, except so far as it clarifies the meaning or intention of the declarative expression on which it depends, as, for example, when it appears to indicate that an expression which is ordinarily assertive has been employed as a suppositive (§3). But such distinctions indicate merely a lack of uniformity, and it is logical that subjunctive usage after declarative expressions employed affirmatively should disappear in proportion to the establishment of a uniform usage of those expressions. An increasing subjection of the language to a uniform rule of practice is reflected in the fact that there are more than two hundred declarative expressions after which no example of subjunctive usage was observed in any of the works examined.

After Negative Verbs

8. We may distinguish three types of negative verbs: ordinary negative verbs or ordinary negation, verbs which are inherently

negative, and verbs occurring in negating circumstances. We shall first consider the case of ordinary negation.

After verbs expressing certainty (type: *savoir, connaître*) mood usage following negation is erratic, but the indicative predominates except in the earlier works of our period:

il n'y a nul icy qui *ne sçache* bien le contraire de vostre dire & qu'il ne *soyt* vrai. (Marg., III, 90)
A tant mit fin à sa menace fière, *Ne sachant* point que c'*etoit* la dernière. (Rons., Fr., 127); à fin que lon *ne sceust* point qu'il *avoit* emporté la ville par trahison (Amy., 103).

9. After perceptive verbs (type: *s'apercevoir, voir* [*voir*, however, being ordinarily a suppositive when employed negatively, and neither being followed by the subjunctive when employed affirmatively]) the subjunctive is predominant when they are negated by either *ne* or *sans:*

s'apercevoir	lire
entendre	trouver
prendre garde	

iamais *n'avez entendu* que i'en *aye* parlé (Marg., III, 201); ilz attendoyent chacun que leur potage vinst, *sans prendre garde* qu'ilz les *heussent* devant eux. (Desp., 15); Nous *ne lisons* point que personne jamais se *soit* desbordé en un contemnent . . . (Calv., R. C., 5); il a été prouvé qu'on *ne trouvera* point en toute l'Écriture que ce mot dormir *soit* attribué aux âmes et esprits (*id.*, O. F., 73); L'on *ne s'est point aperçu* qu'il *ait* pris que cent quatre-vingts pistoles. (Malh., III, 338)

The indicative is exceptional:

Comme si nous *n'entendions* point que c'*est* la finesse de Satan, se transfigurer en Ange de lumiere. (Calv., R. C., xx)

10. After suppositive verbs the subjunctive is the rule:

être assuré (Rab., P., 25-66)[5]	faire accroire (Mont., III, 397)
s'assurer (Mont., I, 42)	estimer
croire	falloir estimer (Est., 180)
pouvoir croire (Malh., III, 47)	se fier (Marg., III, 149)
savoir croire (Rons., Fr., 9)	pouvoir s'imaginer (Vair, 73)
vouloir croire (Paliss., 28)	vouloir s'imaginer (Malh., III, 252)
penser faire croire (Malh., III, 87)	juger

---

[5] Frequently, for brevity's sake, a single example is referred to, without quoting and without mention of further examples.

falloir juger (Calv., O. F., 130)	pouvoir persuader (Malh., III, 153)
penser	trouver
falloir penser (Vair, 136)	voir

je *ne crois* pas qu'il *soit* bien aisé (Malh., III, 65); il *n'estima* point que leur folie luy *tournast* à malheur (Amy., 81); nous *n'estimons* pas que la chose le *vaille*. (Malh., III, 420); celluy . . . *ne iugeroit* que en vous il y *ayt* une telle malice que aux hommes. (Marg., III, 11); Et *ne pense* pas, non, que si les accoustrements sont d'un coquin, que lesprit *soit* lourdaut. (Fail, P. R., 99); Ie *ne treuve* poinct, Madame, dist Saffredent, qu'il *soyt* une plus grande necessité (Marg., III, 44); Or, je *ne vois* point que *puissiez* rien demander en ce passage (Calv., O. F., 103).

The indicative is very exceptional:

nous *ne croyons* pas ou à nostre jugement, ou à celuy des aultres, que l'Escriture *est* de Dieu (Calv., R. C., 21).

In the following century Vaugelas brands the use of the indicative as a not uncommon mistake (Vaug.-Chass., II, 402).

In works later than that of Commynes negative *cuider* rarely occurs:

Ie *ne cuide* pas . . . qu'ils l'*ayent* fait par une theorique imaginative (Paliss., 337).

Consequently, we cannot completely parallel the comparison of *croire*, *cuider*, and *penser* in §2. Among 42 occurrences of negative *croire*, 24 are followed by a subjunctive form, 16 by an indeterminate form, and 2 by the indicative. In the case of negative *penser*, 25 are followed by a subjunctive form, 24 by an indeterminate form, 4 by a subjunctive form employed with conditional force, and 1 by the conditional.

11. After verbs of the assertive type usage is erratic, but the indicative occurs considerably less often than the subjunctive.

accorder	pouvoir dire (Est., 89)
affermer (Calv., O. F., 92)	vouloir dire
concéder (Calv., O. F., 32)	pouvoir s'excuser
vouloir conclure	pouvoir objecter
confesser	parler
vouloir confesser (Est., 139)	porter
dire	reprocher (Calv., O. F., 101)
ouïr dire (Vair, 123)	faire semblant (Marg., III, 129)*

je *n'accorde* pas que leurs prédictions *soient* certaines (Calv., O. F., 128); Je *ne veux conclure* qu'on *doive* effacer du rang des poëtes un grand nombre de Grecs et Latins (Rons., Fr., 7); ie *ne confesseray* iamais qu'aucun tremblement de terre se *puisse* faire sans feu (Paliss., 150); *Il n'est pas dit* que tous en *ayent* usé (Comm., I, 128); Je *ne dy* pas qu'il *soit* vray (Desp., 59); je *ne dicts* pas que ce *soit* relascher son ame, je dicts que c'est la roidir (Mont., III, 439); ie *ne veux pas dire* par là, que la vertu salsitive de la terre sallée *soit* d'un sel commun (Paliss., 349); ils *ne se peuvent excuser* qu'ils ne *soyent* coulpables de sa mort. (*id.*, 105); Et *ne* nous *peut-on pas objecter* pour cela que nous *soyons* moins respectueux . . . (Vair, 169); il *ne parle* poinct que les femmes *ayent* mis les mains à l'ouvrage de Dieu. (Marg., III, 171); La loy . . . *ne porte* pas que nous ne nous *devions* couvrir . . . (Mont., I, 53).

Vous *ne dictes* pas . . . que . . . les bonnes gens de village . . . *avoient* tels predicateurs . . . (Marg., I, 252); ie *ne t'ay point dit*, que toute l'eau . . . se *convertissoit* en pierre (Paliss., 41); Qu'on *ne* me *die* point que *c'est* une medecine trop cher vendue (Mont., III, 419); vous *ne direz* pas que je *suis* paresseux. (Malh., III, 365); France, III; *id.*, 277.

12. After verbs denoting expectancy the subjunctive is the rule:

il fault que vous . . . vous deliberiez . . . ne me chercher . . ., *ny esperer* que ie *puisse* ou *vueille* iamais changer ceste opinion. (Marg., I, 130); *Ne vous attendez* pas que j'*aille* m'amusant à recognoistre mon pous . . . (Mont., III, 421).

13. The dependent clause may be attributive in construction:

avoir connaissance (§8) être du bruit (§11)
y avoir signe (§9) (Desp., 62) sans espoir (§12) (Marg., II, 99)
avoir opinion (§10) (Paliss., 9)

Mais, . . . si *n'est-il point de bruit* que vous *ayez* faict aulcun acte digne . . . (Desp., 323); je *n'ay* encore *cognoissance* bien certaine qu'aucune viande me *nuise* (Mont., III, 431).

14. No occurrences of the subjunctive, except the pluperfect form employed with conditional force, were observed after the following expressions:

falloir alleguer (Est., 34) être mal dit (Calv., R. C., 763)
s'adviser (Comm., I, 131) être expérimenté (*id.*, R. C., xxxiv)
considérer (Vair, 139) se prendre garde (Desp., 20)
être à croire (Marg., III, 91) ramentevoir (Vair, 127)
falloir dire (Calv., O. F., 132) sentir [comprendre] (Mont., III, 380)

15. Two forces, which circumstances bring into opposition occasionally, are at work in connection with declarative verbs employed negatively. The first is a tendency to employ the indicative in relating actual facts, regardless of the construction. The second is a tendency to employ the subjunctive after negative construction. Both are nearly general tendencies. In the case of the declarative expression it is the second which predominates during our period.

After Verbs Inherently Negative

16. In this classification it is necessary to consider separately affirmative, negative, and interrogative construction. In the first division we find *vouloir ignorer, nier, douter, avoir doute*, and *effacer l'opinion* followed by the subjunctive:

tu *veux ignorer* qu'il y en *aye* en toutes terres. (Paliss., 31); je *nie* que le principal *vienne* de là. (Calv., O. F., 114); Le tout fut faist ainsi que avoit esté deliberé, excepté que Gargantua, *doubtant* que on ne *trouvast* à l'heure chausses commodes pour ses jambes, doubtant aussy de quelle façon mieulx duyroient audict orateur, . . . (Rab., G., 20-23); La *doute* que j'*ai* qu'il ne la *sache* pas . . . (Malh., III, 255); *Effacez* de l'esprit des peuples cette *opinion*, que ce Royaume se *puisse* legitimement transferer en une race estrangere (Vair, 125).

The sense of *vouloir ignorer*, as employed here, is *vouloir nier*. There was probably a greater amount of such assimilation than is recognizable. After *ignorer* we find the indicative:

ils *ignorent* que la vraye richesse *gist* au contentement (Marg., II, 4); Froiss., II, 75.

Further research shows that mood usage after affirmative *ignorer* is erratic (cf. Brun., *Hist.*, II, 444), just as it is after negative *savoir*. Mood usage after this class of expressions, however, is predominantly subjunctive.

Douter affirmative does not yet, in this period, belong truly to this class of expressions. It retains its previous sense:

Mes je *dot* mout, que je n'i *faille* (Chr., 773); il deüst dire au duc qu'il n'eust nulle *doubte* ne *craincte* que son maistre *habandonnast* le duc de Guyenne (Comm., I, 232); Ne *doubtez*-vous point qu'il ne vous *ait* baillé quelque aultre pierre . . .? (Desp., 322); on *doute* qu'il ne se *rompe* tout à fait. (Malh., III, 187)

Se douter, previous to our period, has this same sense, expressing fear or apprehension:

Mout par *se doute* l'emperere Li valez ne *soit* baretere. (Gaut., 715); Lors *se douta* que de force li rois de France ne le *renvoiast* en Engleterre (Froiss., II, 35); il *s'apensa* et *doubta* fort qu'elle ne *pourcachast* ce qu'elle faisoit, et . . . que il n'en *fust* destruis. (*id.*, II, 36)

During our period, however, it is already employed with its modern sense:

me doubte fort que le chemyn que vous avez faict la nuict vous *ayt* plus faict de mal que celluy du iour (Marg., II, 121); le paige . . . *se doubtant* que l'on le *cherchoit* (*id.*, II, 41); lui qui *se douta* que c'*étoit* de vouloir voir Madame sa femme (Malh., III, 183); je *me doute* qu'il ne *soit* encore ici (*id.*, III, 17).

Douter is employed secondarily with this same sense (*se douter*) during our period:

on *doubtoit* bien qu'ilz ne *feroient* point tout ce que nous vouldrions (Comm. II, 164); Elisor . . . *doubta* qu'elle le *vouloit* esloingner (Marg., II, 95); ie *doubtois* que vous *estimissiez* gloire en moi, . . . (*id.*, I, 110).

These new employments inherit the old mood usage, producing erratic results. The subjunctive remains predominant, but the indicative is not infrequent.

17. In negative construction we have the following expressions to consider, which correspond logically to §§1, 2, and 3:

(1) ignorer		ôter de la tête
pouvoir ignorer		savoir ôter de la tête
(2) douter	(3) contester	
devoir douter	nier	
falloir douter	falloir nier	
pouvoir douter	pouvoir nier	
y avoir doute	vouloir nier	

This correspondence extends to mood usage only partially. Mood usage after the three groups is erratic, with the subjunctive predominant:

(1) Je *n'ignore* pas que la condition du calamiteux estat où nous avons vescu n'*ait* entamé bien avant la fortune de plusieurs d'entre vous (Vair, 193).

Ie suis seure que vous *ne ignorez* poinct que la fin de tous noz malheurs *est* la mort (Marg., II, 171).

(2) Je *ne doute* point que vous n'*aimiez* l'ouvrage, car je sais trop comme vous aimez l'ouvrier (Malh., III, 23); je *ne doute* pas que plusieurs ne *soyent* de son opinion (Est., 87); *ne doubtez* poinct que . . . le peché *soit* iamais imputé. (Marg., I, 128); *Ne doutez* point que je ne *fasse* tout ce que je pourrai (Malh., III, 37).

ne fault doubter que nul jour ne se *passoit* sans perte ou gaigne (Comm., I, 60); Mon ami, *asseure* toy de cela, *n'en doute* point, que le premier qui fit decouper ses chausses, *estoit* naturellement fol (Paliss., 94).

(3) ie *ne nie* point qu'il n'y *ait* signification (Calv., O. F., 128).

les Italiens diront avoir des façons de parler pour exprimer ceste proposition, . . . : et je *ne* leur *nieray* pas qu'ils en *peuvent* avoir (Est., 116).

We find the indicative also after negative *dissimuler*, and after *doute* occurring in the negating circumstances of *mettre hors de doute:*

Elle . . *ne dissimulloit* poinct à son mary qu'elle *avoyt* des serviteurs (Marg., III, 105).

Nous *metons hors de doubte*, qu'il y *a* en l'esprit humain d'une inclination naturelle quelque sentiment de divinité (Calv., R. C., 4).

18. After interrogative construction we find the subjunctive. The interrogation is ordinarily oratorical, implying negation:

Doubtons-nous que Antechrist *doive* là avoir son siege? (Calv., R. C., xxxi)

Me *sçauroit-on nier*, que ce que ie dis ne *soit* vray? (Paliss., 93)

In summary, mood usage after inherently negative expressions is predominantly subjunctive but also erratic, with some tendency to indicative usage after negation.

After Verbs in Negating Circumstances

19. Quite as we have done previously, we shall consider here five types of verbs or expressions, corresponding to (1) certainty, (2) perception, (3) supposition, (4) assertion, and (5) expectancy. Although this method of division has imperfections, they are counterbalanced by its convenience as a manner of classification.

Among the types enumerated we find the subjunctive employed after the third and fourth when they are negated by the context:

(3) *J'avois de la peine à croire* que deux hommes de si basse condition . . . vous *fussent* plus considérables que je ne suis (Malh., III, 579); *cela est indigne du sens commun de croire* qu'il vous en *veuille* (*id.*, III, 381); *il n'y a lieu de penser* que la vie et menage de tous deux ne *soit* miserable. (Fail, Eutr., 257); *il ne fault pas que vous estimiez* qu'entre nous religieux *soyons* hommes. (Marg., II, 62); *il n'est pas facile de persuader* à plusieurs . . . qu'il leur *faille* obeir (Calv., R. C., 775); *il a esté impossible de persuader* à nos peres que les conquestes faites par vive force . . . ne *fussent* plus advantageuses, que . . . (Mont., I, 67); *nulle des fontaines naturelles ne sçauroyent produire eaux desquelles on puisse estre asseuré* qu'elles *soyent* bonnes (Paliss., 172).

The syntax of this last example follows a broad sixteenth-century practice on which Vaugelas based the rule, considered somewhat ridiculous by Thomas Corneille in 1687, that if the first of three verbs in a continued period be negative, the two following must be subjunctive (Vaug.-Chass., II, 92). In the example cited *puisse* results from the negative antecedent. We find the same mood usage after a superlative antecedent:

Il n'y a que les fols qui se laissent persuader que ce corps dur et massif qui se cuyt en nos roignons se *puisse* dissoudre par breuvages (Mont., III, 420).

In other examples the negative context follows rather than precedes the declarative expression:

pour t'*asseurer* ny *croire* qu'elles *puissent* servir à toutes maladies, *ie suis logé bien loing d'une telle opinion.* (Paliss., 153); de *penser* que le Roy d'Espagne vous *puisse* mettre une grande et puissante armée . . ., *les enfans mesmes ne le croyent plus.* (Vair, 85); D'*estimer* qu'il *soit* en la puissance de cette compagnie d'y apporter la guarison, *c'est nous flatter et, nous flattant, nous tromper.* (*id.*, 35)

We find the same mood after adverbial negation:

il n'est pas difficile de croire qu'il se *puisse* trouver de la terre lemnie. (Paliss., 350)

The subjunctive is not invariable:

je me dispenserai de croire que ma prière ne lui *sera* point inutile. (Malh., III, 26); Mont., III, 349 (indic. & subj.); Vair, 88.

20. Examples having assertive verbs:

(4) *une femme* . . . *se garde bien de dire* qu'elle *ayt* esté priée (Desp., 59); *c'est une cavillation trop impudente de dire que Jérémie confesse* obliquement qu'il y *ait* signification aux astres quand il les nomme signes. (Calv., O. F., 123); *C'est doncques reverie et mensonge, de dire* que l'Eglise *ait* la puissance de juger (*id.*, R. C., 20); *cela ne sert de rien pour approuver* que ce *soit* un art licite. (*id.*, O. F., 129); Je ne doute point que les autres langages . . . ne *facent difficulté d'avouer* ce que j'ay dict, que le nostre . . . se *soit* proposé l'imitation des Grecs (Est., 195).

De *dire* que cela se *doive* tolerer en une ville . . . et qu'elle *puisse* subsister en un tel desordre, *c'est contre tout sens commun* (Vair, 57).

In this last example, as in some of those quoted in §19, construction is somewhat analogous to inversion, in which the subjunctive is commonly employed. When the order of the sentence is regular, adjectival qualification appears to have no effect on the mood of the dependent or attributive clause:

C'est une folle opinion, que tant les Espagnols que quelques autres particuliers *ont conceuë,* que cette couronne se *pouvoit* transferer . . . , et que chacun d'eux la *pouvoit* obtenir (Vair, 125).

After Interrogative Verbs

21. Here we are forced to distinguish oratorical from ordinary interrogation, and to make such further distinctions as the study of contexts may show to be possible. Ordinary interrogation is employed in two differing sets of circumstances: (1) when the speaker is uncertain or when the question implies no definite knowledge on his part; (2) when the speaker already possesses a definite knowledge. In the first case mood usage is erratic. In the second case we do not find the subjunctive, but rather the indicative, or, under certain conditions, the conditional.

(1) M'asseurez vous que vous l'*avez* espousée? (Marg., II, 50); pensez vous, à vostre advis, que les amours des anciens se *demenassent* comme celles de aujourdhuy? (Fail, P. R., 78); Verray-je plus que ma Naiade *sorte* Du fond de l'eau pour m'enseigner le port? (Rons., A., 47)

(2) Croirois tu bien que j*ay* voulu affermer son gaing d'un jour de Pasques trois francs? (Fail, P. R., 102); Et si ie vous en nommois une bien aimante, . . . advoueriez vous que la chose veritable *seroyt* possible? (Marg., I, 96)

This last example is one of a frequently occurring type, illustrating a general tendency of the language to retain the same mood throughout a series of clauses depending each upon the preceding one, that is, illustrating a generalized variant of Vaugelas' rule (§19), which was to fall into disfavor between 1647 and 1687. Further examples of its application may be observed in §3.

22. Oratorical interrogation is employed in three sets of circumstances, the second of which does not differ greatly from the first: (1) when the speaker implies an opinion in the negative; (2) when the speaker implies an opinion and a response in the negative; (3) when the speaker implies an opinion and a response in the affirmative. In the first and second cases mood usage is erratic. In the third, which corresponds somewhat to the second in §21, we do not find the subjunctive.

(1) Et cuides tu que les eaux des pluyes ne *puissent* passer au travers desdits gazons, ou pour mieux dire, que les terres les *boiroyent* . . . ? (Paliss., 179); Comment cuides-tu qu'un laboureur *cognoistra* les saisons de labourer, planter ou semer, sans Philosophie? (*id.*, 16); Pensez-vous qu'il *faille* aller à l'escolle pour l'apprendre? (Desp., 126); Pensez-vous qu'il *faict* beau veoir ung tas de gros veaux perdre tout le temps de leur vie à chercher des petites pierres . . . ? (*id.*, 324); pensoit-il par cela qu'il *reconnoîtroit* le bénéfice après la mort, en ses champs fabuleux? (Calv., O. F., 100); Pensez-vous, quand un tel schisme seroit formé, . . . que vous *feussiez* en seureté? (Vair, 182); O . . . pauvres gens, estimez vous que la peste *vienne* de sainct Sebastian? (Rab., G., 45-39); voudriez-vous que deux grands Princes *fussent* amis, ayans telle maille à partir? (Vair, 78); Ha, monsieur, . . . quelle esperance puis ie avoir que vous *fassiez* pour moy une chose difficille . . . ? (Marg., III, 200)

(2) Cuydez-vous que ung prince mal saige . . . *congnoisse* venir celle malle fortune de loing . . . ? (Comm., II, 229); qui nous asseurera, qu'elle *a* esté gardée en son entier jusques à nostre temps? (Calv., R C., 19); Qui m'assureroit que le goust ouvert que j'ay ce matin je le *retrouvasse* encore à souper? (Mont., III, 433); Qui dira qu'il y *ait* loy au monde, ny divine ny humaine, qui nous *tienne* liez . . . ? (Vair, 175); Avez vous iamais oy dire ne veu que i'*aye* eu amy ne serviteur? (Marg., II, 273); Où avez vous veu . . . que nous *ayons* pourchassé les chamberieres de noz femmes? (*id.*, I, 83); Qui nous peut promettre qu'il n'y *aura* point de division apres sa mort . . . ? (Vair, 181)

(3) Et ne sçavez-vous pas que les garnisons . . . y *ont* esté introduictes
. . .? (Vair, 140); Ne voit-il pas à l'œil que ce *seroit* sa ruine . . .? (*id.*, 76);
ne voyent-ils pas bien . . . qu'il *faudra* qu'ils quittent la place? (*id.*, 79);
Ne voyez vous pas bien . . . que la terre . . . *est* desirée . . .? (Marg., II,
15); ne crois tu pas que le Medecin prudent, n'*ordonnera* iamais une medecine à un malade, si . . . (Paliss., 167); ne jugeront-ils pas qu'il y *va* du
leur . . .? (Vair, 83); T'ay-ie pas dit, que . . . elles *estoyent* diminuees . . .?
(Paliss., 40); ne veut-il pas signifier que l'âme *est* survivante après la mort?
(Calv., O. F., 41); ne leur puis-je pas repliquer que la nostre *a* faict le
mesme? (Est., 17)

23. It may be remarked that the formula of the conditional
sentence, or its mood or tense sequence, tends to remain intact;
and also, that when the construction requires the subjunctive
instead of some other mood, it is the imperfect subjunctive that
replaces the conditional. Among interrogative sentences it is
after the negative-interrogative construction that we find mood
usage most consistent. Generally speaking, an interrogative construction is followed by a mood in conformity with its sense.
Uncertainty and implied negation are followed by the subjunctive,
while implied affirmation is followed by some other mood.

After Conditioned Verbs

24. In connection with verbs expressing certainty we find both
the subjunctive and the indicative, the subjunctive being predominant but tending to become less so:

si ie *congnois* que ce que vous m'avez dict *soyt* vray (Marg., III, 193);
s'il *connoit* qu'elle luy *soit* profitable. (Mont., III, 388)

si les Princes et autres superieurs *congnoissent* qu'il n'y *a* rien plus aggre-
able . . . (Calv., R. C., 762); *s*'il *sçavent* que nous *sommes* assemblez pour
le faire (Vair, 139); Gaut., 399 & Chr., 1176 (*savoir* with subjunctive).

25. Likewise after perceptive verbs usage is erratic:

si tu *vois* une annee qu'il [quelque arbre de Serisier, Pommier, ou Prunier]
n'*aye* guere de fruit, et que le temps se porte sec, tu trouveras ce fruit là
d'une excellente saveur (Paliss., 32); qui pourroit s'en excuser et ne s'en
empescher point, *sinon que* on *veïst* que eulx mesmes y *entendissent* bien et
eussent affection à la matière, seroit bien saige. (Comm., I, 92); *si* . . . vous
jugez . . . que leur delivrance se puisse moyenner . . . *et* davantage vous
recognoissiez qu'elle *puisse* servir comme . . . (Vair, 43); Gaut., 4109
(*voir* with subjunctive).

D'autre part tu ne peuz pas clairement le comprendre, *sinon que* tu *re-congnoisse* qu'il *est* la fonteine et source de tout bien. (Calv., R. C., 6); *si* nous *entendons* que le Magistrat, en punissant, ne *faict* rien de soy, . . . ce scrupule ne nous agitera pas fort. (*id.*, R. C., 761); Gaut., 3773 (*entendre* with subjunctive).

26. After suppositive verbs the subjunctive is usual, and the indicative is exceptional:

si vous *croyez* que ce *soit* chose qui le mérite. (Malh., III, 196); *S'*il est permis de *croyre* . . . Que . . . Humain esprit de soy *puisse* advenir A . . . (Rab., G., 58-5); Mais *si* vous *pensez* que les finesses dont chascun vous pense bien remply *soient* plus grandes que celles des femmes, ie vous laisse mon rang (Marg., I, 71); Que *si* quelcun *pensoit* que les Grecs . . . *eussent* compris aussi la fauconnerie, il s'abuseroit (Est., 119); *Si* quelqu'un *estime* que . . . j'*aye* mal trié cettuy-ci, . . . (Mont., III, 365); et en ferez faire une pour nous, *si* vous *jugez* qu'ils le *vaillent*. (Malh., III, 42)

Sages, *s'*ils *eussent creu* que c'*estoit* là leur ordinaire vacation (Mont., III, 439); Toutesfois *si* quelqu'un vouloit de ce *inferer* qu'on ne *doibt* obeissance sinon à un juste Seigneur, il argueroit perversement. (Calv., R. C., 780); France, 14 (*croire* with indic.).

27. After assertive verbs we find both the indicative and the subjunctive, but in works later than the *Heptaméron* the indicative occurs more frequently than the subjunctive:

Et *s'*il y a homme ou femme qui veuille *dire* que iamais i'en *aye* parlé, . . . (Marg., I, 25); *Si* celuy qui c'est *pretend* que je luy *aye* faict tort . . . (Desp., 119); Chr., 6559 (*vouloir dire* with subj.); *id.*, 2433 (*respondre* with subj.).

Et *si* tu me *dis* qu'il *combat* trop tost . . . (Rons., Fr., 12); *si* tu *dis* que entre les montaignes et la mer il y *peut* avoir quelques subtiles aspirations . . . (Paliss., 168); *S'*ils *disent*, non-obstant ceci, que la pesle se *veut* moquer du fourgon, . . . (Est., 79); Indicative: *alléguer* (Calv., O. F., 114); *arguer* (*id.*, R. C., VI); *proposer* (*id.*, R. C., 16); *objecter* (Fail, Eutr., 299); *écrire* (Paliss., 166); *accorder* (Est., 35); *confesser* (*id.*, 81).

Likewise after concessive conjunctions:

combien que nostre Seigneur *testifie*, que le Magistrat *soit* un don . . . (Calv., R. C., 776); *encore que* nous *accordions* que l'âme *soit* prise pour la vie (*id.*, O. F., 51); Et *encore que* je *confesse* qu'il se *soit* trouvé des gouverneurs et capitaines, qui . . . (Amy., XIV).

Au reste, *encore que* je *confesse* que les autres nations *ont* aussi bien des ars, . . . (Est , 139).

28. We have noted a tendency to increase the employment of the indicative and decrease the employment of the subjunctive, after affirmative declarative verbs (§§1-4). We may say that this same tendency exists also after conditioned declarative verbs, but that it is uniformly retarded. In one group, the assertive verbs, conditional *si* is beginning, early in our period, to cease to affect at all the mood of the dependent clause. In the other groups the subjunctive in the dependent clause may result from uncertainty or implied negation rather than from the mere extension, to the dependent verb, of the contingency resulting from the conditional employment of the main verb. We may look upon it, however, in all groups, as a sort of mechanical extension of modality, if we duly consider the fact that most of the conjunctions synonymous with *si*, and *que* in a second protasis, are followed by the subjunctive. The displacement of the subjunctive by the indicative, after conditioned assertive verbs, appears to constitute one of the earliest breaks in the rule or practice of extended modality, examples of which have been noted in §§3, 19, 21, and one phase of which was to be formulated by Vaugelas nearly a century too late to enjoy complete favor.

Rules in 1618

29. Let us examine the rules which may be drawn, interpretatively, from the second edition of Maupas' grammar (283-299). We may expect some change from preceding usage. For example, Maupas allows this choice:

> I'aimerois bien un cheval qui *allast*,
> ou qui *iroit* l'amble.

But, from Gautier d'Arras to Malherbe, in this type of sentence, the subjunctive occurs in the works examined approximately one hundred times as often as the conditional.

According to Maupas, verbs expressing certainty, perceptive verbs, and assertive verbs are followed by the indicative, but if negative, interrogative, or conditioned, they are followed by either the indicative or the subjunctive. For the affirmative Maupas' rule is in line with the movement of the preceding century;

but for the other cases the findings reported above rarely show a tendency for mood usage to remain indifferent.

Suppositive verbs, along with which Maupas lists inadvertently a few expressions of emotion, are followed, according to him, by the indicative or the subjunctive, indifferently. This is more or less true, according to the verb involved, as we have seen. When negative, interrogative, or conditioned, they may be followed by the indicative, says Maupas, but he adds that the subjunctive [*optatif*] is *plus vif & de meilleure grace.* Here again his opinion is apparently not based on a definite knowledge of established major precedents.

The past tenses of verbs denoting expectancy, he says, are followed by the conditional. This accords with the tendency of the preceding century.

Turning from Maupas' grammar to Malherbe's *Commentaire sur Des Portes* (Malh., IV, 249-473), we find this difference between them: that Malherbe's corrections are invariably made in conformity with the major practice of the preceding half-century. Malherbe appears to possess the rare faculty for distinguishing, even at close range, the *insines exemples e vrai uzaje* which Pierre de La Ramée, in 1562, had pointed out as the true ornaments of the language.

IN SUBJECTIVE CLAUSES

Affirmative

30. The subjunctive is very exceptional with expressions of affirmative sense affirmatively employed. It may ordinarily be traced to inversion:

Pour exemple: que ce mot Pointe *soit* un ancien terme des mariniers, *il appert* par le livre mesmement qui est intitulé, . . . (Est., 134); Mont., I, 59.

Et qu'il *soit* vray qu'il *ait* sagement contenu les forces des Atheniens au dedans de la Grece, *les effects le tesmoignent* (Amy., 36); Que cela *soit* vray, *nous en avons de trop funestes exemples* chez nous pour nous mettre en peine d'en chercher en l'antiquité (Vair, 177).

These last two examples contain variations of a formula of long usage:

Et, *que il soit vray*, ne a-il pas en mariage dame Marguerite, . . .? (Froiss., XV, 280); *id.*, XV, 160.

Qu'il soit vray. Voicy depuis, de nouveau, que les plus legers mouvements espreignent le pur sang de mes reins. (Mont., III, 421)

This formula, which is utilized generally to introduce the proof of an assertion, occurs less often than *qu'ainsi soit*, employed for the same purpose:

Or qu'ainsi *soit* que quelques-uns en abusent, *il appert* par la controverse qui est entr'eux (Est., 85); Et *qu'ainsi soit*, long temps y-a qu'un distique de Martial fut traduict en ceste sorte de vers. (*id.*, 41)

Qu'ainsi soit, prenez . . . quelc'un de ces jeunes gens du temps present, . . . (Rab., G., 15-12); Calv., O. F., 112.

Palissy prefers *qu'ainsi ne soit:*

Qu'ainsi ne soit, contemple un peu les vins de Montpellier, ils ont une puissance et force admirable (Paliss., 20); *id.*, 21.

Palissy's construction becomes common, and Vaugelas complains that it is employed in a sense contrary to its negative form (Vaug., 557). But not only is it an example of the tyranny of usage versus reason, as Vaugelas points out; it is also an example of detached employment of an element of inverted construction.

31. Ordinarily, expressions which report, affirm, or imply belief are followed by the indicative, the future, or the conditional. Such are:

il y a	c'est chose veritable
c'est une chose apparente	il se trouve
il advient	il vient
il est ainsi	(la) vérité est
il appert	il se voit
il arrive	il est vrai
il est certain	
il (c') est chose certaine	(il) me souvient
il s'ensuit	
il est évident	il se coule un bruit
il est manifeste	il court un bruit
il est notoire	
il paraît	c'est quelque conjecture

il est à croire	il vient en fantaisie à qlqn
il est aisé à croire	il vient en pensée à qlqn
il est croyable	

Il y a davantage que telz personnages ne *peuvent* pas facilement sortir (Amy., xx); *il est ainsi,* que les fumees de toute espece de bois, *font* cuire les yeux (Paliss., 21); *il s'ensuivra* aussi que nostre nation *ha* un plus grand preparatif à l'eloquence qu'aucune des autres. (Est., 10)

The mood may vary with the force of the expression:

il s'ensuit [it follows necessarily] que le nombre des termes qui les doivent accompagner *soit* plus grand. (Est., 150)

32. In construction in which the subordinate clause appears as a predicate[6] stating a fact, numerous introductory expressions capable of implying emotion or volition (incumbency, necessity, compulsion) are employed to state opinions about that fact; that is, they are employed merely as elements of a declarative sentence and are not followed by the subjunctive when so employed. Some of these expressions are:

Marg.: il est bon (I, 84); c'est grande chose (III, 159).
Rab.: le bon feut (P., 14-65).
Calv.: c'est fraude et trahison (R. C., vii); c'est une chose mauvaise (O. F., 75); c'est le propre (R. C., xxxv); c'est force et violence (R. C., vii); c'est une chose ordinaire et commune (O F., 85); reputoit cela estre un grand vice (R. C., xxx).
Paliss.: c'estoit une grande ignorance (168).
Amy.: le pis est (xix).
Est.: reputé pour un grand heur (8); est une chose esmerveillable (129).
Mont.: il est bon (III, 85).
Vair: chose estrange (191).
Malh.: l'importance est (III, 374).

C'est fraude et trahison, que sans cause elle *est* notée de sedition et malefice. (Calv., R. C., vii); Car *il est bon* que les mots qui sont le . . . mieus teuz, *sont* les mieux sceus (Mont., III, 85); *c'est une chose ordinaire et commune* en l'Écriture que cette vie éternelle et bienheureuse *est* signifiée par ce mot de

---

[6] Under the heading of objective clauses may be found examples of clauses employed attributively and as predicates, and occasional examples of clauses employed after impersonal expressions. Since it is improbable that any one would be misled by inclusions not strictly within the boundaries of a given class, such inclusions are practised wherever they appear to be pertinent.

résurrection (Calv., O. F., 85); Gaut.: *Granz aventure est* (1378), *Confaite chose* . . . ! (3240), *C'est* . . . *coustume* (2009).

Except in the employment described above such expressions are followed by the subjunctive, e.g.: Comm., I, 3 (*c'est chose accoustumée*); Marg., III, 61 (*il seroyt bon*); Calv., O. F., 80 (*ce seroit une chose absurde*); Fail, P. R., 67 (*il sera bon*); Mont., I, 57 (*c'est une ceremonie ordinaire*); Vair, 133 (*quelle detestation*); Gaut., 6465 (*est chascuns coustumiers*).

Non-affirmative

33. The term "non-affirmative" may be applied to expressions which do not imply certainty and are equivalent to expressions of opinion. Such are:

il semble	il y a de l'apparence
il semble à qlqn	il est vraisemblable
il semble avis	il est veriforme

An isolated occurrence of *il est veriforme* (Rab., P., 6-42) is followed by the indicative. The subjunctive is exceptional after *il est vraisemblable* (Est., 36, following *poser que*): compare its usage after *il semble vrai* in France, 157. Calvin and Estienne employ the subjunctive after *il semble avis* and *il y a apparence*, respectively, but Estienne also employs other moods. Turning back to the twelfth century for a comparison, we find erratic usage after *il est vis à quelqu'un*, in Chrétien's work.

After both *il semble* and *il semble à quelqu'un*, usage is erratic:

et *semble* que les jésuites *sont* beaucoup déchus de leur crédit (Malh., III, 182); et *semble* que depuis la volonté qu'il en avoit *soit* refroidie (*id.*, III, 228); France, 282, 135.

Il me semble qu'il *est* temps (Marg., I, 45); *me semble* que ce *soyt* folye (*id.*, II, 237); Malh., III, 61, 184.

Distinct tendencies exist, however. After *il semble* the subjunctive is predominant before Commynes, and tends to remain so. After *il semble à quelqu'un* the indicative is predominant before the time of Commynes, and remains predominant. Let us examine the mood frequency tables:[7]

[7] See p. 7, note 2.

Key to columns: number of occurrences followed by (1) indicative; (2) future; (3) conditional; (4) indeterminate verb form; (5) subjunctive; (6) subjunctive employed with conditional force.

sembler	(1)	(2)	(3)	(4)	(5)	(6)
Gaut.	—	—	—	—	1	—
Chr.	—	—	—	2	5	—
Froiss.	—	—	—	—	2	—
Comm.	5	—	—	11	14	3
Marg.	7	—	—	15	3	—
Rab.	—	—	—	4	2	—
Desp.	—	—	—	3	2	—
Calv. O.F.	1	—	—	1	2	—
R.C.	—	—	—	1	3	—
Paliss.	6	—	—	1	4	—
Amy.	4	—	—	5	2	—
Est.	1	—	2	—	2	—
Mont.	2	—	—	3	11	—
Vair	1	—	—	6	8	—
Vair (Var. *D*)	—	—	1	—	—	—
Malh.	1	—	—	—	—	—
Malh. (outside of III, 1-202)	—	—	—	—	2	—
France	1	—	—	—	3	—

sembler à qlqn	(1)	(2)	(3)	(4)	(5)	(6)
Chr.	2	—	—	—	4	—
Froiss.	8	—	2	—	2	—
Comm.	44	2	22	8	—	2
Comm. (Var. *A*)	—	—	—	—	1	—
Marg.	63	5	8	12	4	—
Rab.	1	—	—	1	—	—
Desp.	11	—	1	—	—	—
Calv. O.F.	3	—	1c[8]	—	—	—
Fail	2	1	2	1	—	—
Rons.	2	—	—	—	—	—
Paliss.	7	—	4	—	—	—
Amy.	2	—	—	2	—	2
Est.	5	1	—	1	—	1
Mont.	2	—	—	—	—	—
Vair	4	—	—	2	—	—
Malh.	2	—	—	1	—	1
France	4	—	1c	—	—	—

[8] See p. 8, note 3.

It will be noted that mood usage in these cases is comparable to that after the suppositives in objective clauses (§2). Generally speaking, however, mood usage after impersonal expressions tends to become settled at an earlier date.

Conceptional

34. It is the opinion of M. Meillet that in the Indo-European languages the subjunctive was originally a future in force and usage.[9] In our period it is convenient to regard the subjunctive as the mood employed to describe what is conceived in the mind and yet remains contingent, that is, to depict the condition of action existing in a formulated state only. We may also regard certain expressions, some of which function as modal adverbs, as being conceptional. They are:

(il) peut être	il peut avenir
il peut se faire	il est possible

All the examples of *être possible* that were observed occur in connection with indirect interrogation and are followed by the subjunctive. For example:

J'entens bien que . . . vous . . . demandez *comment est il possible* que ainsi *soit* (Rab., P., 1-158).

The other expressions are followed by the indicative, the future, or the conditional. For example:

Peut-estre que la misericorde de Dieu le *convertira* (Vair, 161); *pourroit estre* qu'ilz *avoyent* esté cruelz et tyrans. (Comm., II, 324); *Peut estre* qu'ilz ne *diroient* chose (Marg., III, 165); *il peut estre* que les sels . . . *pourroyent* endurcir . . . (Paliss., 153); *Il pourroit* bien *estre* que . . . ilz *auroient choisy* . . . (Desp., 315); *se pourroit faire* que . . . *se pourroit* aulcune chose *trouver* qui . . . (Comm., I, 2); *il pourra advenir* que . . . il *usera* de retranchement (Est., 47); *il peut advenir* que fortune vous le *fera* souffrir un jour (Mont., III, 359); Chr.: Mes *puet cel estre* an nul androit Ceste pucele ne *voldroit,* Que fusse suens et ele moie. (2325)

Compare:

je le pourrois bien dire avec plusieurs autres, et *possible* que cela ne seroit point trop mal dit (Calv., O. F., 36).

[9] A. Meillet, *Esquisse d'une histoire de la langue latine* (Paris, 1928).

Although these expressions occupy the place of a main clause, they function as modal adverbs modifying the verb of the subordinate clause. Eventually, a division is to take place: on one hand, *il est possible que* (and *il se peut que*) followed by the subjunctive, but reverting, in the form of *c'est possible* (and *cela se peut*), to Chrétien's construction; and on the other hand, *peut-être que* having no effect on the mood of the following clause, and displaying its adverbial nature when *que* is removed, through an inversion which leaves it no longer separated from the verb by the subject of the sentence.

From the use of the modal adverb *peut-être* with the indicative or primary and ordinary form of the finite verb it is but a step to the use of *pouvoir* and *devoir* as modal auxiliaries supplying the sense of subjunctive usage without appearing in the subjunctive form. Indicative forms of these verbs occur during our period in examples whose authors employ, in the same construction, the subjunctive forms of all other verbs. And in the following century Vaugelas, for example, considers that *ie parlois assez haut pour qu'il m'entendist* is equivalent to *ie parlois si haut qu'il me pouvoit bien entendre.* In addition to the verb *pouvoir*, expressing possibility, and the verb *devoir*, expressing futurity, we have also to consider the verb *avoir*, which, after having provided the endings of the future tense, also expresses futurity when joined to the infinitive through the conjunctive preposition *à*. This consideration brings us again to M. Meillet's opinion concerning the original sense of the subjunctive in the Indo-European languages, but we need not go back farther than the twelfth century to find examples demonstrating both that the future tense is essentially comparable to an infinitive accompanied by a modal auxiliary and that in this sense it is equivalent to the subjunctive:

> Dont m'*estuet il* que je lour *die,*
> Ou que je li *face* gehir. (Gaut., 2329)

> *El* li *estuet* que chastée
> *A estre* tel com il demande
> Et com li sire li commande. (*id.*, 2549)

Other examples demonstrate the displacement of this twelfth-century subjunctive by the future:

Lasse! or ne sai dont que je *face*. (Gaut., 3610)

je ne sçay pas que *pourra faire* le pauvre peuple (Vair, 55).

In our period the future is used in many constructions or circumstances in which the other forms of the indicative are not employed. This is the reason for considering it separately.

Elsewhere we have noted the extension of modality (§§3, 19, 21, 28). Here we note the transfer of modality to modal adverbs in the guise of conceptional expressions and to modal auxiliaries.

Inherently Negative

35. The subjunctive is general after expressions of inherently negative sense, such as *être difficile, impossible, incertain, malaisé*:

il est bien difficile que celuy qui est fort doux se *puisse* monstrer fort grave (Est., 89); aucuns se moqueront, en disant qu'*il est impossible* qu'un homme destitué de la langue Latine *puisse* avoir intelligence des choses naturelles (Paliss., 130); *il sera malaisé* qu'ils le *fassent* croire (Malh., III, 103).

In Negating Circumstances

36. The subjunctive is general:

à grand poine voit on advenir que grans bancqueteurs *facent* beaulx faictz d'armes. (Rab., P., 27-69)

à grant peine se peult-il faire qu'il n'y *ait* de l'envye (Comm., II, 257).

This last construction is interpretable also as *faire* volitional, as a consecutive construction preceded by negation, or as *que* for *sans que*, owing to a following negative. Such examples of the syntactical unity of the language are not rare.

Negative

37. The subjunctive is likewise general after negated expressions corresponding to those in §§30, 31, 33, 34, 35:

(§30) qu'ainsi ne soit
ce n'est pas

qu'ainsi ne soit, qu'il *n'*y *aye* de l'eau dedans les pierres, considere celles qu'on fait cuire pour faire la chaux, . . . apres qu'elles sont cuites, elles sont legeres. (Paliss., 41)

il ne fut iamais que les bonnes inventions ne *fussent* recompensées par les Roys (Paliss., 6); Et, par ce qu'*il n'est* pas qu'un jour quelqu'un n'*ayt* ceste grace de . . . (Desp., 50); Jamais au cuœur *ne sera* que je n'*aye* . . . Le souvenir (Rons., A., 143); être en paradis et vivre avec Dieu, *ce n'est* point que . . . l'un *soit* ouï de l'autre (Calv., O. F., 100); Gaut., 6356.

Construction in this last group must not be confused with (1) negated causative construction, (2) construction in which *si* is elided, or (3) construction in which the negation applies only to an adverbial expression, e.g.:

(1) *ce n'est pas* que mon logis ne soit fort aisé à trouver (Malh., III, 59).

(2) Il fust pieça homme fait pour certain, *N'estoit* qu'il craint ceste male putain. (Amy., 40)

(3) ce n'est pas *de maintenant seulement* qu'il a pris naissance (Calv., O. F., 27).

(§§ 31, 33)

il n'y a apparence	il n'est pas vrai
il n'est nul apparent	il n'est pas vraisemblable
il n'advient	il ne souvient pas à qlqn
il ne s'ensuit	il ne semble pas
il ne reste	il ne semble pas à qlqn

(§ 34)
il ne peut être
il ne peut se faire
il n'est pas possible

il ne peut estre qu'elles ne *soyent* sans comparaison meilleures (Paliss., 142); *il ne peut se faire* que nous ne *concevions* une fantaisie que . . . (Calv., O. F., 122); *Il n'est pas possible* que je *récrive* tant de fois une même chose. (Malh., III, 128)

Preceded by negation:

Car *je ne voy point* comment *il est possible* que deux personnes . . . se *puissent* tellement accorder (Est., 70).

(§35)
il n'y a nulle doute
il n'y a point de doute

il n'y a nul doute que le prophète ne nous *veuille* ramener . . . (Calv., O. F., 121); *il n'y-a nulle doute* qu'il ne *soit* . . . offensé (Est., 148).

Without effect on the formula of the conditional sentence:

si j'avois à vous en prier aussi bien de bouche comme par lettre, *il n'y a point de doute* que j'*aurois* de la peine à m'y résoudre. (Malh., III, 353)

Interrogative

38. The subjunctive is the rule:

Comme *va* cela, dit Lupolde, que de si peu de chose . . . se *puisse* produire tant de corps ensemble? (Fail, Eutr., 285); Comment, je vous prie, *est-il croyable* qu'une si grande Princesse . . . *ait* peu porter ceste extreme misere . . .? (Vair, 14); *Vous semble-t-il* que ceste espée *soit* belle & bonne? (Marg., I, 233); *vous semble-t-il avis* que Job et David *aient* exposé les âmes aux vers pour les manger? (Calv., O. F., 73); *est il possible* que vostre beaulté *soyt* sans amy . . .? (Marg., III, 202); Gaut., 4951.

The indicative is very exceptional:

Est il bien *possible* que vous *avez* trouvé vostre seur en l'estat que vous dictes? (Marg., II, 86)

Negative-Interrogative

39. Usage varies; we find both the subjunctive and the indicative, but not after the same expression:

Vous semble il pas que ceste femme . . . *ait* vertueusement resisté? (Marg., I, 145); *N'est-il pas possible* que j'*aye* cette femme-là? (Desp., 175) *Te souvient-il pas* que i'*ay* assemblé . . . (Paliss., 352).

Conditioned

40. The subjunctive is general:

s'il est ainsi	si tant est
si ainsi est	s'il advient
s'il est vrai	s'il semble à qlqn

Ilz iurerent tous dire verité *s'il estoit ainsi* qu'ilz ne la *peussent* denyer. (Marg., III, 34); *Si ainsi est* que la mine de fer *ait* telle vertu, il se trouvera . . . (Paliss., 154); *si tant estoit* que ces pieces . . . *eussent* tant d'efficace que vous dictes. (Desp., 320); *si tant est* que tu *vueilles* justement administrer . . . (Amy., xxɪɪ); *Si vous semble* que je vous *aye* faict . . . service agreable (Rab., G., 52-9); *S'il advient* que je *sache* une foys cela (Desp., 317); *s'il est vray* que dans tous les cœurs des hommes bien nez la nature *ayt* imprimé un charitable amour . . . (Vair, 127).

Palissy also employs *si ainsi est* with the sense of *puisque ainsi est*, with the indicative:

Or *si ainsi est*, que les arbres et autres vegetatifs *travaillent**, et *sont* malades en produisant, il faut conclurre, que . . . (30).

After *quand il adviendroit* he employs both the pluperfect subjunctive and the past conditional (121).

41. Generally speaking, the differentiation between indicative and subjunctive usage in subjective clauses after declarative expressions is very distinct during our period. The line of demarcation passes between whatever is real or a fact and whatever is less than real or a fact.

There is a noteworthy tendency towards brevity and fixed employment of expressions. The impersonal expressions incline to become shorter, and their sense tends to become more sharply defined in usage. *Chose,* in expressions such as *c'est une chose apparente, certaine, croyable, véritable,* etc., is much less often employed after the time of Amyot than before. This is true also of *ainsi* for *vrai,* especially in the expressions *qu'ainsi soit, qu'ainsi ne soit,* and *comme ainsi soit.*

Il semble and *il semble à quelqu'un* are, at the beginning of our period, already more frequently employed than *il pert* and *il pert à quelqu'un.* Early in our period they become fixed in meaning and employment. *Il arrive, il s'ensuit,* and *il se trouve* appear, while *il advient* and *il vient* lose no ground.

In contrast with usage after other declarative expressions usage after the impersonal expressions is well established and shows less tendency to be erratic. Their sense and employment appear to be more firmly fixed. They resist assimilation and, as may be noted in the case of *sembler* and *sembler à quelqu'un,* they also resist dissimilation.

RÉSUMÉ

42. It would be impossible to generalize concerning declarative expressions taken by and large. In order to generalize at all it has been necessary to break up the general body of declarative expressions into small groups. These groups are brought together again in the table below, which shows the state and tendencies of modal syntax after declarative expressions during our period.

Key: I, indicative; Se, subjunctive exceptional; Ip, indicative predominant, still predominant, or becoming predominant; E, erratic; Sp, subjunctive predominant, still predominant, or becoming predominant; Ie, indicative exceptional; S, subjunctive.

Objective clauses

	I	Se	Ip	E	Sp	Ie	S
Majority of affirmative expressions	*						
Perceptive, affirmative	*						
Certainty, interrogative (oratorical) . . .	*						
Certainty, affirmative	*	*					
Suppositive, affirmative			*	*			
Assertive, affirmative			*	*			
Expectancy, affirmative			*	*			
Certainty, negative			*	*			
Certainty, conditioned			*	*			
Assertive, conditioned			*	*			
Perceptive, conditioned				*			
Perceptive, interrogative				*			
Suppositive, interrogative				*			
Assertive, interrogative				*			
All types above, negative-interrogative . .	*						
Assertive, negative				*	*		
Certainty antonyms, affirmative				*	*		
Suppositive antonyms, affirmative				*	*		
Certainty antonyms, negative				*	*		
Suppositive antonyms, negative				*	*		
Assertive antonyms, negative				*	*		
Perceptive, negative				*			
Suppositive, negative						*	*
Suppositive, conditioned						*	*
Assertive antonyms, affirmative							*
Suppositive antonyms, interrogative (oratorical)							*
Assertive antonyms, interrogative (oratorical)							*
Suppositive, in negating circumstances							*
Assertive, in negating circumstances							*

Subjective clauses

	I	Se	Ip	E	Sp	Ie	S
Expressions which report, affirm, or imply belief, affirmative	*						
Descriptive expressions, implying an opinion, applied to a fact, affirmative . .	*						
Expressions of affirmative sense, affirmative	*	*					
Conceptional expressions, affirmative . .	*						*
Non-affirmative, with personal dative, affirmative			*	*			
Non-affirmative, impersonal, affirmative				*	*		
Conceptional, interrogative						*	*
Expressions of affirmative sense, negative							*
Report, affirmation, implied belief, negative							*

	I	Se	Ip	E	Sp	Ie	S
Report, affirmation, implied belief, interrogative							*
Conceptional, negative							*
Non-affirmative, with personal dative, negative							*
Non-affirmative, with personal dative, interrogative							*
Non-affirmative, impersonal, negative							*
Expressions occurring in negating circumstances							*
Conditioned							*
Inherently negative expressions, affirmative							*
Inherently negative expressions, negative							*

43. We know that mood usage is largely a matter of inherited manners of expression, and we may assume that its development is subject to analogy. We perceive, also, that its variations may result from exterior causes: assimilation; attraction, or the extension of modality; transfer of modality; tendency of the present conditional form to displace, within certain limits, the imperfect subjunctive form; persistency of the formula of the conditional sentence; inversion. From some of Maupas' statements (§29) we understand, furthermore, that mood usage is somewhat a matter of style.

We have noted that Maupas places declarative verbs and expressions of emotion in the same list: e.g., *croire, s'étonner*. To this list he adds *autres de mesme sens où y a esmotion d'esprit entre asseurance, & incertitude*. This indication of a threefold classification (expressions of certainty, of uncertainty, and of something between these extremes) constitutes a grammatical advance, but it is also an accident rising from his intention to systematize the study of French syntax for foreign students. On the other hand, his failure to differentiate between classes is indicative of the amount of assimilation between them, and of the degree of attention which modal syntax had received. Whether this failure is due to the syntax of the two classes being essentially the same, and to the lack of any indication that it is going to change (Brun., *Hist.* III, 570), is a question to which an answer may be found in the next chapter. Here we conclude by noting that, although there is much erratic mood usage after declarative expressions, there are comparatively few cases in which examination does not disclose some distinct major tendency.

CHAPTER II

AFTER EXPRESSIONS OF EMOTION

IN INDIRECT INTERROGATION

44. As the first step in examining modal syntax after expressions of emotion, let us note that certain expressions of emotion are employed in the manner of declarative expressions. These are expressions of wonderment or astonishment employed in indirect interrogation. We find successively:

se merveiller que	to wonder what (Chr., 3017)
s'émerveiller comme	to wonder how (Gaut., 1642; Marg., I, 172; Amy., 61)
s'émerveiller qui	to wonder who (Froiss., II, 81)
s'émerveiller comment	to wonder how (Froiss., II, 36)
s'émerveiller pourquoi	to wonder why (Froiss., II, 35; Calv., R. C., vii)
s'ébahir de quoi	to wonder why[1] (Comm., I, 78)
être ébahi comme	to wonder how (Comm., I, 28)
s'ébahir comme	to wonder how (Comm., II, 286; Marg., II, 179; id., III, 223)
s'ébahir comment	to wonder how (Comm., II, 73; Marg., II, 170; Rab., P., 11-58; Desp., 327)
s'ébahir pourquoi	to wonder why (Marg., II, 237; Calv., O. F., 48)
s'ébahir dont	to wonder whence (Marg., II, 273; Amy., xxi)
être émerveillé comment	to wonder how (Desp., 326)
être ébahi que	to wonder what (Desp., 117)
s'étonner comme	to wonder how (Mont., III, 403)
s'étonner si	to wonder whether (Vair, 20)

These constructions are followed by the indicative.

THE INDICATIVE

45. A few citations will serve to illustrate this section of the history of indicative usage after expressions of emotion. We find wonder or astonishment expressed successively by:

[1] This expression is also employed with the meaning "to be astonished that."

37

venir à merveille à quelqu'un que (Gaut., 1657)
être émerveillé de ce que (Froiss., XV, 155)
s'ébahir que (Comm., II, 239; Marg., I, 89; Desp., 36; Fail, P. R., 73;
    Rons., A., 86; Est., 94)
s'émerveiller de ce que (Marg., II, 40)
s'émerveiller que (Marg., III, 28; Est., 28)
être ébahi que (Desp., 104; Fail, P. R., 117)
faire ébahir à quelqu'un de ce que (Malh., III, 115)
être étonné que (Malh., III, 295)

From the employment of the conjunctive locution *de ce que* it is apparent that the indicative is employed to express the cause of the emotion. We find also the following expressions, after which the indicative is used:

Gaut.	en avoir le cœur amer que
	se douloir pour ce que
	avoir le cœur éjoui de ce que
	en avoir le cœur irascu que
Chr.	se courroucer de ce que
Comm.	se mécontenter de quoi
Marg.	être aise de quoi
	être aise dont
	avoir pitié dont
	être scandalisé de ce que
Rab.	se contrister de ce que
	grever à quelqu'un de ce que
	être marri de ce que
Malh.	être piqué de ce que
	se piquer de ce que

Since we are dealing with what was primarily a causative construction, we may assume that the use of the indicative after *que* indicates merely that *que* is employed as a causal conjunction, while the use of the subjunctive indicates that the construction is in a state of transition.

IN OBJECTIVE CLAUSES

Affirmative Construction

46. The expressions and usages occurring in the works examined are tabulated on the following pages.

Key: I, indicative; S, subjunctive; E, erratic, indicative and subjunctive.

	GAUT.	CHR.	FROISS.	COMM.	MARG.	RAB.	DESP.	CALV.	FAIL	RONS.	PALISS.	AMY.	EST.	MONT.	VAIR	MALH.	FRANCE
ressentir une affliction de ce																	S
être aise					E		E		I					I		E	
être aise de quoi				I													
être aise dont				I													
(être aise de savoir)							S										
en avoir le cœur amer	I																
recevoir une consolation												S					
être content								S				S					
se contenter				I		I								I			
se contrister de ce						I											
se courroucer de ce	I																
craindre	S	S	S	S	S	S		S			S	S		S	S		S
(craindre qu'on ne dise)														I			
crainte															S		
être en défiance				S													
déplaire à qlqn					I												
se douloir															S		
se douloir pour ce	I																
douter	S	S	S														
se douter	S	S															
être dueuz de qlqn ou de qlch	I																
être ébahi									I								
faire ébahir à qlqn de ce																I	
s'ébahir				I	I		I		I	I			S				
s'ébahir de quoi				I													
avoir le cœur éjoui de ce	I																
être émerveillé								S									
être émerveillé de ce			I														
s'émerveiller					I									I			
s'émerveiller de ce					I												
ennuyer et grever à qlqn	I																
enragé															S		
s'esmai(i)er	S																
être étonné																I	
s'étonner																S	
trouver étrange				E					E				S				
se fâcher								S								E	
gratifier à qlqn														E			

	GAUT.	CHR.	FROISS.	COMM.	MARG.	RAB.	DESP.	CALV.	FAIL	RONS.	PALISS.	AMY.	EST.	MONT.	VAIR	MALH.	FRANCE
grever à qlqn ce	I																
grever à qlqn de ce				I													
se sentir heureux														S			
se tenir heureux																S	
avoir honte				S													
en avoir le cœur irascu		I															
être liez		I															
être malheureux		I															
être marri								E						S		E	
être marri de ce				I													
trouver mauvais de ce												I					
se mécontenter de quoi				I													
s'offenser																S	
pouvoir être pesanz		I															
peser à qlqn ce	I																
avoir peur	S		S	S	S	S	S			S				S		S	
être piqué de ce																I	
se piquer de ce																I	
avoir pitié dont				I													
être la pitié				I													
quelle pitié!														S			
plaindre														S			
se plaindre		I														I	S
prendre plaisir																S	
regret																S	
avoir regret														E			
regretter				I												E	S
se réjouir																S	
se repentir			S														
être scandalisé de ce				I													

These expressions are not all employed invariably with a uniform sense: e.g., *être aise* (ironical): consentir (Marg., II, 49); *se contenter:* s'assurer, croire (Marg., I, 16; Desp., 81); *avoir peur:* croire, se douter (Malh., III, 79). It is probably unnecessary to call attention to the essentially declarative nature of expressions denoting fear and implying uncertainty and sometimes unwillingness; but it should be noted that mood usage after them is especially constant. Similarly, expressions of pleasure or displeasure may be indirect expressions of volition.

As our period opens the usage of the subjunctive is practically limited to those cases in which the action of the subordinate clause is anticipated, that is, where it is merely formulated and is not existent either previously to, or simultaneously with, the action of the main clause. The subjunctive is limited, also, to occurrence after expressions containing an element either of uncertainty or of volition. This distinction between clauses appears, therefore, to be a conscious one, rising from the analytical treatment of conjunctive locutions and forming a corollary to the analytical treatment of antecedents which is reflected by the persistence of the relative clause in dependent construction. The passing of this distinction corresponds to the general tendency toward simplification or reduction of conjunctive locutions introducing dependent clauses, although, after certain expressions in this particular category, *de ce que* continues to be used.

47. We have already noted the apparent reason for indicative usage (§45). It remains to see at what point the subjunctive begins to appear in clauses expressing the actual present or past cause of the emotion. In our authors the subjunctive in clauses expressing cause is very rare up to the time of Des Périers:

vous . . . *avez* incontinent *trouvé estrange* que ie *parlasse* à ung gentil homme aussi malheureux en ceste vie que moy (Marg., II, 45); Gaut., 660 (*se repentir* implying volition).

In and after Des Périers, examples are less rare:

furent bien *aises* que les deux s'en *allassent* (Desp., 90); Et *suis esmerveillé* qu'il ne se *soit* encores trouvé roy, . . . qui . . . (*id.*, 222); Du bastard . . . qui se laissoit pendre . . ., et qui *se faschoit* qu'on le *sauvast* (*id.*, 133); Il *est marry* . . . que tu luy *ayes* respondu «un poullet» (*id.*, 53).

Tu *trouves* bien *estrange*, que ie *dise* qu'il y a du sel en toutes especes de pierres (Paliss., 33); Et me *gratifie* . . . que cette correction me *soit* arrivée . . ., et que je me vois desfaict de cette maladie (Mont., I, 80); Je *plains* qu'on n'*aye* suyvy un train que j'ay veu commencer (*id.*, III, 405); vous voyez . . . les estrangers . . . *enragez* que ceste proye leur *soit* eschappée des mains (Vair, 197); je . . . *m'étonne* bien qu'il *ait* pris cette résolution (Malh., III, 117); je *me réjouis* que vous *soyez* de retour (*id.*, III, 97).

Having observed this fact, we are brought to the question of how subjunctive usage becomes extended to clauses expressing the cause.

48. The answer to this question is arbitrary in some respects, but perhaps satisfactory. Let us begin by comparing Gautier d'Arras' construction with Malherbe's:

Gaut.: Mout par [li senescauz] *est liez* de grant maniere Qu'il [Eracle] se *prouva* si en le piere (1333).

Malh.: Je *suis* bien *aise* que vous *fûtes* bien accommodé à la carrouselle (III, 2; in 1606).

Malh.: Je vous envoye une dernière douzaine d'exemplaires, mais c'est d'une impression faite sans mon sçu et sans mon aveu. Je m'*en* suis, au commencement, *offensé* à bon escient; mais à cette heure . . ., je *suis* bien *aise* que cette commodité se *soit* offerte de satisfaire à mes amis qui en desirent avoir. (III, 579; in 1628)

It is hardly probable that the thought processes differ in the cases of the two authors, or in the cases of the two examples from Malherbe. Now let us note the constructions in which the indicative is employed. In our authors up to and including Rabelais, the construction frequently contains *de ce*, *pour ce*, *de quoy*, or *dont*. Let us trace the sense of this *ce*, which is *this fact:*

Or *ce* que j'ay promis de declarer, par quelles Loix doibt estre gouvernée une police Chrestienne, n'est pas que je veuille entrer en longue disputation, à scavoir, quelles seroient les meilleures Loix. (Calv., R. C., 766)

on est moult esmerveillié en son pays de *ce* que il veult prendre la fille de son adversaire en mariage (Froiss., XV, 155).

d'*une chose* ay grant merveille que nous n'oons de monseigneur le roy . . . nulles nouvelles (*id.*, XV, 249); Le duc . . . considéra *une chose* que ce voyage . . . cousteroit trop grandement (*id.*, XV, 225).

In proportion as the frequency of these constructions diminishes in favor of the more general employment of *que* alone, there appears to come into the language a confusion of clauses introduced by *que* and depicting the action contingent to that of the main verb, with clauses introduced by *que* and presenting the cause. This results in the employment of the subjunctive after *que* causative. The confusion appears to extend in both directions, so that finally instead of the logical

Cil a le cuer mout esjoï *De çou que* Deus l'*a* si oï (Gaut., 6412);

or

Le moyne . . . se contristoit merveilleusement *de ce qu'*il ne les *povoit* secourir. (Rab., G., 44-4);

we find

Le saint homme Maël ressentait une profonde affliction *de ce que* les premiers voiles mis à une fille d'Alca *eussent* trahi la pudeur pingouine, loin de la servir. (France, 57)

In other words, the subjunctive in clauses expressing the cause appears to be a constructional accident which became firmly fixed in the language of the sixteenth century: the substitution of an objective clause for a causative adverbial clause, owing to their mechanical similarity. Or, we may say, it is merely a special manifestation of a general tendency of the subjunctive to attach to *que*, just as *que* attaches to the subjunctive.

We may not presume that, once the adverbial clause has been generally supplanted by the objective clause, the subjunctive any longer expresses the cause. We may presume, rather, that a new manner of speaking has been established, which presents the action of the dependent clause as being contingently related to that of the main clause. This may be called a new syntax.

49. The future and conditional forms also are found after expressions of emotion, e.g., after *avoir peur* and *craindre:*

Future: Marg., III, 70; Paliss., 97; Malh., III, 79.
Conditional: Comm., I, 170 (conditional sentence); Marg., II, 261 (conditional sentence).

Negative Construction

50. The subjunctive occurs after:

craindre	s'étonner
avoir crainte	trouver étrange
se défier	avoir peur
s'émerveiller	regretter
être étonné	se soucier

Et *n'ayez pas paour* que i'en *sceusse* aymer d'aultre (Marg., I, 140); Je *ne suis pas étonné* qu'elle *die* . . . (Malh., III, 222); Ceux donc qui sçauront ces choses, *ne s'esmerveilleront* point que vostre Majesté *prenne* plaisir au present Discours (Est., 8); Afin que vous *ne vous étonniez* pas que la prise de la citadelle de Mézières *ait* été faite en si peu de temps (Malh., III, 400).

The indicative occurs in causative clauses, even after negation:

Ie *ne trouve poinct estrange* . . . *de quoy* la parolle *ensuict* le faict (Marg., III, 141); Et *ne faut point qu'aucun s'ébahisse* que les saints Pères . . . *étoient* en chartre. (Calv., O. F., 42)

Interrogative Construction

51. Examples:

Trouvez vous estrange que une princesse nourrie en tout honneur *soit* difficile à prendre d'un seul homme? (Marg., I, 60); Et *pensez vous*, dist Nomerfide, que les hommes *se soucient* que l'on le *sçache*, mais qu'ils viennent à leur fin? (*id.*, III, 165)

IN SUBJECTIVE CLAUSES

52. Strictly analyzed, emotion unmingled with approval or disapproval is rare. We may say that it is confined to wonderment, surprise, or astonishment, and that these terms define the proper limits of this chapter. The expression of any other emotion may imply pleasure or displeasure, and so may be, in a sense, an expression of volition. All expressions of emotion, however, are reactions to either a past or a present fact, or, if there is anticipation, to an idea:

> Si lour en prent mout granz peeurs
> Que cil ne die lour couvine (Gaut., 2137).

In cases of the latter type the expression indicates a supposition and so in this sense is related to the suppositive declaratives. But, however closely these two groups may be related, in sense, to their neighbors in the preceding and following chapters, the relationship does not extend to modal syntax except in a minor and an accidental manner.

53. Facts, as we have frequently noted, tend to find expression in the indicative:

C'est dommaige, dist Oisille, qu'il ne *s'adressa** . . . (Marg., I, 242); *C'est dommaige* . . . dont vous *avez* une femme de bien (*id.*, II, 133); Gaut., 1086; Froiss., II, 144.

At the same time we find contingent conditions expressed in the subjunctive:

seroyt grand dommaige . . . que ceulx qui ne vous ayment peut estre poinct en *fussent* heritiers. (Marg., II, 177)

The observation of construction is more important, however. We observe that the variety of constructional accidents tends to decrease, thus leaving a sort of standardized practice. We see also that this standardized practice occurs earlier in the case of the subjective clause than in the case of the objective clause. The subjective clause, unlike the objective clause, is rarely introduced by *de ce que, pour ce que, de quoy,* or *dont.*

In subjective clauses a standardized practice appears to have been achieved by Rabelais' time, and the subjunctive becomes general:

Grecque sans laquelle *c'est honte* que une personne se *die* sçavant (Rab., P., 8-72); *il me fasche bien* qu'elle *devienne* si vieille (Desp., 87); *n'est-ce pas grand pitié* que deux si grands personnages . . . l'*ayent* employé à des disputes . . .? (Est., 19); *Il est bien advenu* que le plus digne homme d'estre cogneu et d'estre presenté au monde pour exemple, ce *soit* celuy duquel nous ayons plus certaine cognoissance. (Mont., III, 341); *Quelle horreur, quelle detestation,* qu'on ne se *contentast* pas de nous faire sevir les uns contre les autres (Vair, 133); *Quelle pitié,* que nous *ayons* veu ces jours passez seize coquins de la ville de Paris faire vente au Roy d'Espagne de la couronne de France . . .! (*id.,* 123); aussi *est-ce un grand malheur* que n'y ayant eu qu'un homme tué, le sort *soit* tombé sur son mari. (Malh., III, 529); *ce lui seroit une grande honte* que la Reine le *trouvât* encore ici (*id.,* 310).

The construction designated in § 45 as a causative construction, or clause presenting the cause, with the indicative, exists both before and after Rabelais, but after Rabelais it becomes exceptional:

Et ne doibt *sembler estrange* que je *remetz* maintenant à la police, la charge de bien ordonner la Religion (Calv., R. C., 755); Et *c'est merveille* que ceux d'Éphèse . . . *ont* brûlé leurs livres (*id.,* O. F., 132); Gaut., 1657.

RÉSUMÉ

54. Syntax is in a state of transition. The indicative is employed in clauses stating the cause. In objective clauses mood usage appears to be erratic, if one subjects it to a merely casual examination. At the opening of our period[2] the employment of

[2] See Chapter I, p. 6, note I.

the subjunctive is practically limited to those cases where the action of the subordinate clause is anticipated. Subjunctive usage increases somewhat during the latter part of the sixteenth century. There is a tendency of *de ce que* to displace *pour ce que, de quoi,* and *dont,* and to be in turn displaced by *que.* In subjective clauses, evidence of transition appears earlier, and the indicative becomes exceptional in the latter part of our period.

At the end of the sixteenth century the language appears to be free from many of its former complexities, and also from some of those doubtlessly convenient simplicities of construction which allowed Gautier d'Arras to write:

> Mout par en ai le cuer amer
> Qu'il ne set com jel puis amer.
> Il nel puet savoir a nul fuer;
> Pour çou ai mout amer le cuer.
> Certes, a gré mout me vendroit
> Pour çou qu'il seüst orendroit
> Le douleur que je trai pour lui.
>   (3928)

CHAPTER III

AFTER EXPRESSIONS OF VOLITION, NECESSITY, ETC.

Affirmative

55. In the present study the term "expression of volition" is used in its broadest sense, following fundamentally the terminology and the classification of expressions employed in Ayer's *Grammaire comparée*. But since Ayer does not classify a very great number of expressions and does not distinguish between affirmative and other constructions, it is necessary greatly to extend and refine his classification, besides, of course, taking into account semantic differences in the expressions actually classified, wherever such differences occur.

Construction after volitional expressions has a wide range, thus making it difficult, even if it were desirable, to establish strict boundary lines. In some cases clauses following these expressions could be construed as clauses of purpose, e.g.:

supplia un sçavant medecin . . . *à ce qu'il considerast* si possible estoit remettre Gargantua en meilleure voye (Rab., G., 23-8). Compare: Pierre Claret luy *supplya que*, pour son acquict, il luy en *signast* une quictance. (Comm., II, 243)

In this connection may be noted Professor Ritchie's opinion that in Old French optative *que* is hardly distinguishable primarily from *que* employed with the force of *afin que* (p. 56). Even as late as Froissart we find examples which tend to substantiate this opinion.

In other cases the volitional expression is employed as a declarative:

Dieu *voulut* [Il arriva] qu'il *trouva* une porte ouverte, qui se rendoit au iardin, auquel il entra (Paliss., 102); mon malheur *voulut* que je n'y *arrivai* qu'après que ce fut fait. (Malh., III, 401)

47

In still other cases the clause may be construed as a consecutive one, after expressions of causation or prevention:

je demanderay aux Pasteurs mon trouppeau . . . et *feray* qu'ils ne l'*auront* plus en garde. (Vair, 187). Compare: ie *feray en sorte* vers mon frere que sa teste *sera* tesmoing de ma chasteté. (Marg., I, 55)—result; *faisons en sorte* qu'avant que l'heure nous prenne et que nous nous levions de noz places, nous *ayons fait* arrest. (Vair, 143)—purpose; *Faictes* donc qu'il ne se *fasse* choix de personne qui ne soit propre . . . (*id.*, 201).

Cela a *empêché* que le siége de Meurs ne s'*est* pas encore fait. (Malh., III, 11); Chr., 5764.

56. Having considered these preliminary matters, we are ready to note the range of direct expressions of volition employed during our period. Nearly half as many more occur in the works of Gautier, Chrétien, and Froissart.

adjurer	garder	prouvoir
aimer	se garder	querir
commander	implorer à ce	recommander
conjurer	insister	requérir
conseiller	instruire	être requis
défendre	instruire à ce	retenir
demander	invoquer à ce	sauver (à ce)
désirer	louer	solliciter
empêcher	obliger à ce	souhaiter
engarder	obtester	supplier
enjoindre	obvier à ce	supplier à ce
éviter	presser	traiter
exhorter	prier	travailler
faire	procurer	vouloir

After these expressions the subjunctive is the rule. The present conditional (after past tenses) and the future (after the present tense) do not occur often, and the indicative is very exceptional.

Zenon *conseilloit* . . . qu'ilz *feissent* les presumptueux (Amy., 8); il *conseilloit*, et *estoit d'advis* que lon *devoit* (*v.* §34) avoir un peu de patience (*id.*, 67).

nous . . . *empescherons* . . . que les bourgeois ne *soient* indeuëment vexez (Vair, 58); Ce qui *empêche* qu'on ne les *voit* point encore, c'est . . . (Malh., III, 499).

Il les *feïst* demourer devant l'ostel . . . et qu'ilz l'*attendissent* (Comm., I, 119); ceux . . . se sont obligez de *faire* que le Roy de Navarre *envoyeroit*

. . . (Vair, 119); je m'en voys *faire* . . . que ce cheval-là *parlera* à son pale-fernier (Desp., 335).

ie vous *prie*, s'il est digne de ceste compaignye, que vous nous le *veulliez* dire. (Marg., III, 83); Ie vous *prye*, dist Simontault, que vous nous le *dictes*. (*id*., III, 12)

ie vous *supplie* que ma iuste requeste me *soyt* octroyée (Marg., I, 112); Ie vous *supplie*, ma dame, dist Geburon, s'il est ainsi que vous *prenez** ma place & que vous le *dictes*. (*id*., I, 230)

On *voulut* que je la *visse* . . .; c'est pourquoi je la vis (Malh., III, 2); La raison *veut* que nous *espousions* . . . (Est., 115); la raison *voudroit* aussi qu'ilz *eussent* plus grande provision . . . (Amy., xix); l'experience de l'antiquité, qui *veut* qu'en matiere d'advis et conseil, il *faut* estre prié et non poursuivant (Fail, Eutr., 216).

57. The formula of the conditional sentence rarely persists after volitional expressions:

leur *priant* qu'ilz taschassent à reduyre ce peuple en bonne paix et que, en cas qu'ilz ne voulsissent à ce entendre, que au moins eulx, recongnois-sans la bonté que on leur faisoit, ne se *trouveroient* en guerre contre luy (Comm., I, 104); ie vous *requiers* que si en avez le moindre sentiment de soupson qui puisse estre, que vous le me *dictes* (Marg., III, 21); ie vous *prie* que après cela si vous avez oppinion de moy & que le me dissimullez ou que le trouvez mauvais, ie ne *demeureray* iamais en vostre compaignye. (*id*., III, 22)

It would not be unreasonable to assume that these expressions are employed in a sense bordering on the declarative. Compare:

les amis de Hannibal luy *conseilloyent* qu'il *suyvist** sa fortune, et qu'il *entreroit* pesle mesle quand et les fuyans dedans la ville de Rome [i.e., s'il la suivait] (Amy., 93).

We do not, however, find the subjunctive after volitional expressions employed declaratively, e.g.:

envoya *prier* le duc de Bourgongne qu'il *peüst* loger au chasteau et que tous ceulx-là qui estoient venuz *estoient* ses malveillans. (Comm., I, 128); la *priant* ne leur faire ceste honte, & que si elle les vouloyt doulcement mener au port, ils luy *promectoient* de ne luy demander rien. (Marg., I, 64); les *suppliant* estre traictez plus humainement, . . . et que jamais envers eulx ne *commirent* excès ne oultraige . . ., et que Dieu les en *puniroit* de brief. (Rab., G., 26-47); la princesse . . . *pria* Mme de Nevers de faire désister M. du Maine . . . et que ce respect . . . se *devoit* garder entre parents si proches (Malh., III, 357).

In other examples the elision of a declarative verb is more evident:

Le bon homme . . . *demandoit* à Jouanne sa femme un petit à boire, . . . & quil *lavoit* bien gaigné (Fail, P. R., 71); il *commandoit* que tout le monde se allast coucher, & quil *feroit* bien son appointement (*id.*, P. R., 75).

Perhaps the most important notation to be made here is that elliptical construction is much rarer after the time of Noël du Fail than in the earlier works examined.

58. Thus far construction involving volitional expressions has been considered from various angles: (1) viewing the dependent clause as a purpose clause; (2) as a consecutive clause of result; (3) as being hindered by the conditional sentence formula; (4) viewing the volitional expression as a declarative; (5) assuming the elision of a declarative expression. None of these considerations deals specifically with examples of expressions of entreaty followed apparently by the second person plural present indicative form (§56), which are not rare. This form seems to be historically identical with the form employed in parataxis, that is, a hypotactic imperative.[1]

Malherbe, correcting Desportes, objects to two constructions which we find occasionally in the works of preceding authors: (1) the use of the subjunctive after any form of *faire* except the imperative (e.g., §§55, 56); (2) the use of one volitional expression dependent on another, e.g.:

me *coniura* que . . . ie *voulusse* changer le nom des personnes (Marg., I, 97); Pericles . . . le *pria* . . . qu'il *retournast en voulunté* de vivre (Amy., 31).

59. The number of volitional expressions presented in §56 is considerably augmented by those belonging to other groups: (1) declarative expressions employed with volitional force; (2) construction in which the dependent clause is attributive; (3) attributive construction after declarative expressions employed with volitional force; (4) construction in which the dependent clause expresses a predicate:

(1)	admonester	adviser
	admonester à ce	affermer

---

[1] As shown in the monograph referred to in the Introduction, p. 3, note 3.

avertir	entendre et vouloir
être conclu	juger
conclure	mander
crier	persuader
faire crier	prétendre
dénoncer	proposer
dire	remonstrer
écrire	répondre
entendre	faire savoir
faire entendre	

raconta l'estat onquel avoit trouvé les ennemys . . ., *afferment* que ilz n'estoient que maraulx . . . et que hardiment ilz [lui et ses compagnons] se *missent* en voye (Rab., G., 36-4); Quand ces beaulx yeulx *jugeront* que me *meure* (Rons., A., 54); il leur a mandé gens pour leur *denoncer* qu'ils n'y *entrassent* point. (Vair, 153)

(2)

faire le bien	avoir l'œil
donner commandement	mettre peine
faire commandement	faire une prière
avoir désir	avoir un procès à ce
avoir envie	faire (une) requête
l'exhortation	présenter requête
prendre garde	avoir (le) soin
se prendre garde	tendre à fin
faire instance	exiger tribut
tenir la main	

Je vous prie, Monsieur, de me *faire ce bien*, que Monsieur le premier président *sache* que je lui baise . . . les mains (Malh., III, 156); je fourmay complainte à la Court contre les mulles . . ., *tendent à fin* que . . . les conseillieres leur *feissent* de belles baverettes (Rab., P., 17-108); Le seul *tribut* qu'il *exige* de vous, c'est que vous *vueillez* estre heureux. (Vair, 192); luy priant qu'il *teint la main* que son maistre *acceptast* ce party (Comm., I, 170).

Compare:

Audit duc de Lorraine promectoit *tenir la main* que ce siège ne s'*avanceroit* point et qu'il feroit trouver des deffaulx ès choses (Comm., II, 136).

(3)

être d'avis	ajouter un point
envoyer une lettre	remonstrances (faites) à ce
venir nouvelles	faire réponse
être d'opinion	faire signe
paroles (dites)	

Et . . . luy *vindrent nouvelles* que . . . ilz se *hastassent* de marcher (Comm., I, 150); ils ont trouvé bon de supplier la Reine d'y *ajouter* [à l'édit des duels] encore trois ou quatre *points*, dont l'un est que la connoissance en *soit* du tout ôtée au prévôt de l'hôtel (Malh., III, 294); Elle lui *fit signe* avec la main qu'il se *relevât* (*id.*, III, 431).

(4)   être le but   être l'opinion
       être la conclusion   être le parti (ouvert)
       conditions (demandées)   être le plaisir
       être la coustume   être le remède
       être la fin   être la volonté
       être l'intention   être la nouvelle (voulue)

Leur *but* est que . . . il se *face* eslection. (Vair, 121); son *plaisir* est que *soit* multiplié (Rab., P., 18-66).

Attributive construction occasionally becomes predicate construction through the interpolation of a relative with *être:*

Et, oultre, luy ouvrit ung party nouveau, *qui estoit* qu'ilz se asseürassent bien l'ung de l'autre . . . (Comm., II, 19).

Predicate construction is occasionally inverted:

les *conditions* que demande M. de Savoie sont que ceux de Genève *désarment**, et que les fortifications nouvelles qu'ils ont faites *soient* démolies. (Malh., III, 228)

A declarative expression is occasionally subject to a preceding volitional expression:

Dieu veuille que la première *nouvelle* que vous aurez de moi soit que Monsieur le légat *ait* avancé quelque chose! (Malh., III, 164)

The conditional is not infrequent after past tenses of expressions of will or intention. This usage is found mainly, however, after expressions denoting a resolution, a decision, or an arrangement.

Negative, Interrogative, or Conditioned

60. Contrary to the case in affirmative construction, we find in these categories no exceptions to subjunctive usage. A few expressions which do not occur in any of the preceding affirmative lists may be added here:

pouvoir empêcher	pouvoir retenir
pouvoir faire	savoir vouloir
garantir	savoir contredire
pouvoir garder	devoir être cause
vouloir requerir	être la volonté telle

Les espritz *ne sceurent contredire* qu'ils n'y *entrassent* (Desp., 46); le bon vouloir que j'ay vers luy, . . . *ne doit pas estre cause* que vous me *laissiez* mourir en vous aimant. (*id.*, 62); Mais *si la volunté* du Seigneur *est telle* que nous *cheminions* sur terre ce pendant que nous aspirons à nostre vray païs: . . . (Calv., R. C., 754).

IN OBJECTIVE CLAUSES

AFTER INDIRECT EXPRESSIONS OF VOLITION

Affirmative

61. In addition to volitional expressions of the direct type we find a large number of the indirect type:

être accordé	trouver mauvais
accorder	
s'accorder	appartenir à ce
être aise	être digne
consentir	se juger digne
donner	mériter
endurer	valoir
octroyer	
permettre	voir
prendre sans déplaisir	
prendre à faveur	faire un accord
prendre à gloire	avoir le bien
souffrir	faire l'honneur
trouver bon	

After expressions of this type the subjunctive is the predominant usage:

Donne, grand Dieu, qu'au milieu de la guerre *Puisse* ruer ses ennemis par terre (Rons., Fr., 75); un gladiateur . . . *endura* tousjours riant qu'on luy *sondat* et *detaillat* ses playes. (Mont., I, 71); Le mesme empereur *print* encores *sans desplaisir* que Virgile l'*appellast* filz d'un boulangier (Desp., 57); Et *prendray* . . . *à gloire* qu'on *die* de moy que . . . (Rab., G., Prol. -83); on *trouve mauvays* que ung simple gentil homme . . . *vienne* à espouser une femme de grande maison (Marg., II, 237); le pauvre peuple *souffroit* patiemment que tous leurs bois *fussent* coupez (Paliss., 103).

Car elle [la police] n'*appartient* pas seulement *à ce*, que les hommes... *soient* substantez en leur vie, . . . mais *à ce* que ydolatrie . . . et autres scandales . . ., ne *soient* publiquement mis en avant (Calv., R. C., 755); la cause . . qui me semble *estre* . . . *digne* que promptement y *donniez* ordre. (Marg., III, 190); un spectacle qui *vaut* bien que l'on *vienne* du bout de la France pour le voir. (Malh., III, 535)

mesmes s'ilz dissimuloient, *voyans* que les Roys desordonnéement *vexassent* le povre populaire, j'estimeroie . . . (Calv., R. C., 782).

il croit que . . . je la vous aye communiquée en cinq ou six mois que j'*ai eu le bien* que nous *ayons* vécu ensemble. (Malh., III, 87); *Faites-moi cet honneur* que je *sache* le coût (*id.*, III, 18).

The conditional is not infrequent when the expression is employed to denote a resolution, a decision, or an arrangement:

leur *fut permis* que tous les iours *assisteroient* . . . (Marg., II, 22); *accorda* le ieune que le plus viel *commenceroit.* (*id.*, I, 63); Il *octroya* que la flotte Troyenne *Pourroit* aller dessus l'onde Egéenne (Rons., Fr., 78).

The indicative is exceptional:

son mary *trouvoit mauvais* qu'elle *avoit* des serviteurs (Marg., III, 105), cf. §§52, 53; Froiss., XV, 216 (*avoir grâce*); Gaut., 5705 (*souffrir*).

Negative, Interrogative, or Conditioned

62. Here again, as in §60, we find no exceptions to subjunctive usage. Additional expressions, not listed in §61, are:

vouloir accepter	vouloir souffrir
pouvoir endurer	prendre à dédain
vouloir permettre	à grand peine vouloir consentir

Ne prenez pas à obstination ou à desdain que . . . je n'*aille* vous suppliant (Mont., III, 363); Compare: nous vous prions de ne trouver point mauvais *si* nous vous en disons . . . (Desp., 17); je *ne trouveray point mauvais* que ceux qui se sentiront estre en meilleur equippage que moy . . ., se *vueillent* mettre en ma place (Est., 14), cf. §§52, 53.

A grand peine voulurent consentir . . . que on luy *portast* deux flascons de vin. (Comm., I, 194)

Doibs je endurer que . . . l'on me *vienne* ratisser et tabuster le cerveau, . . .? (Rab., P., 12-14)

Que si vous *trouvez bon* que je *dye* ce que luy ay veu faire autresfois, je mettray peine me y acquitter. (Fail, P. R., 148)

IN OBJECTIVE CLAUSES

AFTER EXPRESSIONS INDICATING A RESOLUTION,

A DECISION, OR AN ARRANGEMENT

Affirmative

63. Expressions of this nature, employed in this manner, occur very frequently in Froissart's work, owing to its character. In it we find them followed by the subjunctive, the present conditional, and, exceptionally, the indicative (e.g., *devoit*). Occasionally the imperfect subjunctive and the present conditional occur together:

Et *fu ordonné* que on *laisseroit* là tous harnois et tous charois, et que casquns ne *presist* qu'un pain et le *troussast* derrière lui. (Froiss., II, 143)

But in Froissart's time the functions of one are not so clearly distinguished from those of the other as they are at the end of the sixteenth century. In the sixteenth century these two forms become less interchangeable, and the conditional gains some ground at the expense of the subjunctive. This is true in the case we are now considering, but only within certain limits which we shall note.

64. In the sixteenth-century works the following expressions fall into this classification, owing to the manner in which they are employed either constantly or occasionally:

être l'accord tel	délibérer
faire un accord	être dit
être accordé	faire publier et passer un édit
accorder	prendre enseignes
être aise (§46; Marg., II, 49)	être établi
être appointé tellement	établir
faire appointement	faire (une) ordonnance
donner arrêt	faire passer une ordonnance
être arrêté	être ordonné
être conclu	ordonner
conclure	ordonner et vouloir
être la conclusion	donner ordre
être constitué	mettre ordre
mettre en avant un décret	être ratifié
proposer un décret	être résolu
être décrété	la résolution s'est prise

After this type of expression we find the imperfect subjunctive or the present conditional, and the present subjunctive or the future:

Grandgousier *ordonna* que Ulrich Gallet . . . *allast* devers Picrochole (Rab., G., 30-3); icelluy . . . *ordonna* qu'il *feroit* à sa maniere accoustumée (*id.*, G., 21-9); ie *ordonne* que vous *soyez* mise . . . (Marg., II, 70); je suis d'advis que la Cour . . . *ordonne* que remonstrances *seront* faictes (Vair, 143).

The employment of the subjunctive in such examples appears to distinguish a wish from a disposition. It seems to differentiate what remains contingent from what it is assumed will occur.

65. The dependent clause is apparently a consecutive one when it contains a form of the conditional or the future. The construction is sometimes manifestly consecutive:

L'accord fut tel que d'icelle lippée Elle en *auroit* deux œufz de Proserpine (Rab., G., 2-72).

But even in this case the subjunctive also occurs:

Tellement fut appointé entre eulx et moy qu'ilz *payeroiont* tout le bestial qu'ilz auroient prins ou le *rendissent* (Comm., I, 210).

In this last example the equality of the subjunctive and the conditional is evident; and from the variants, *paièrent* and *rendirent*, in the Polignac manuscript, the consecutive nature of the construction is evident. Purely consecutive construction after volitional expressions is not, in fact, extraordinary, e.g.:

Dieu *voulut ainsi* disposer des choses que ceste nuyct sourdit une grande tormente (Comm., I, 200); Dieu *voulut tant* de bien à ce roy qu'il estoit logé près de la mer (*id.*, I, 202).

Examples of past tenses of the indicative after volitional expressions (§55) belong, essentially, in this same category, distinguishing facts from contingencies. Or, we may consider that facts, past, present, and future, are the will of the Deity or its agents, the king, providence, or chance; and that volition in such a case is fact, neither contingent nor uncertain, neither possible nor impossible, but merely accomplished or to be accomplished. By extension, the wish of a king or a governing body will become a fact with the passing of time. Henri Estienne states that the bidding of the king is imagined as having already been done, as soon as he has spoken, whereas another's bidding would be held to have merely been expressed. He indicates that this is especially true of a French king, as is shown by an old proverb (Est., 4-6).

Estienne's statements and his modal syntax bear no logical relation to each other. His statements are related, however, incidentally and accidentally, to the syntax of Amyot. In Amyot's work the subjunctive is ordinarily employed after expressions such as *faire passer une ordonnance, être ordonné, ordonner,* and *donner ordre:*

Pericles estant en la fleur de son credit avoit fait passer une ordonnance, que ceulx la seuls *fussent* tenus pour bourgeois d'Athenes, qui seroyent nez de pere et de mere Atheniens (Amy., 60).

But when the subject is a governing body rather than an individual, and when the order has the nature of a final decision from which there may be no appeal, the subjunctive is not employed:

Le senat ordonna que lon n'*envoyeroit* point d'argent pour les delivrer, et blasma grandement Fabius (Amy., 78); *id.,* 108.

66. Amyot is the first among our authors who appears to make this choice consciously. This fact is significant for the history of the modern grammatical rule concerning mood usage in such cases. At the same time the historical significance of the employment of the conditional and the future in such cases can be drawn from an examination of the following examples:

Il *seroit* autrement, *mien vueil.* (Gaut., 3575); Et *mon vuel* toz jorz le *verroie* (Chr., 923); O que *volontiers* i'*aimeroye* (R. Est., 1558). Compare: Et *à la mienne volunté* que chascun *laissast* sa propre besoigne (Rab., P., Prol.-10).

Mais ja n'i *mourra* qu'uns, *suen vueil.* (Gaut., 5595); ja nel *leissera son vuel.* (Chr., 6078). Compare: *A la mienne volonté,* qu'un chacun qui verra ce secret, *soit* . . . soigneux à le garder (Paliss., 24).

Mar i *avra* cop feru plus. (Chr., 4966); Ia ni *aura* homme qui die . . . (Gaut., 5020: variant *T*). Compare: Ja *mar soit* nus hom qui çou die . . . (Gaut., 5020); Tu *besongneras* six jours, et *feras* toutes tes œuvres. Le septiesme est le repoz du Seigneur (Calv., R. C., 144).

This lingering optative employment of the conditional and the future finally becomes converted into what is to all intents and purposes a consecutive construction. In the second half of the sixteenth century we still find the subjunctive, the conditional, and the future, but the last two ordinarily occur only after those expressions which belong to the language of a governing body or final authority. At that time both usage and construction tend to become more stabilized.

Negative or Conditioned

67. In these categories we find no exceptions to subjunctive usage:

ne le peut-on résoudre qu'il ne *meure* dans peu de temps. (Malh., III, 363); *si* à aulcun, après avoir eu des ennemis victoire, *estoit decreté* qu'il *entrast* à Rome en estat triumphant, . . . (Rab., G., 10-57); Froiss., XV, 275 (pouvoir conclure ou accorder qlqn qu'il . . .); II, 41 (faire une alliance).[2]

SUPPLEMENTARY OBSERVATIONS

Obtenir

68. The entire range of mood usage after the volitional expressions may be found after *obtenir*, which contains the properties of both a causative and a volitional expression: *faire qu'il soit permis* or *se faire accorder.* For example:

Et toutesfois, par telle veneration de son sepulchre, ilz *obtenoient* qu'ilz *estoient* gueris de morsures de serpens. (Calv., R. C., xx)

tout ce que lon *peut obtenir*, ce fut que les premiers *demeureroient* (Vair, 117); ils *ont obtenu* . . . qu'ils ne *seroient* plus tenus de . . . (Malh., III, 393).

M. du Maine *a obtenu* du Roi que M. d'Elbeuf *fera* sa charge de grand chambellan. (Malh., III, 164)

la puissance des adversaires de Dieu *a obtenu* jusques là, que la verité de Christ . . . *soit* cachée et ensevelie (Calv., R. C., ix); ils *veulent obtenir* . . . qu'elle *soit* réduite à néant. (*id.*, O. F., 67); (France, 292).

si par les prières il *ne peut obtenir* que l'on *fasse* justice, il sera contraint de recourir aux armes. (Malh., III, 516)

Typical Expressions

69. *Vouloir, permettre, faire* (except when it is followed by a consecutive clause of result), *empêcher, trouver bon, trouver mauvais, prier, commander, dire,* and *ordonner* may be considered repre-

---

[2] Note the similarity of the expressions employed by Froissart (XV, 275) and Malherbe (III, 363). Only the latter, however, could be classed with those shown in § 10.

sentative expressions in the several categories. The table below presents the mood frequency totals for our authors from Commynes to Malherbe inclusive, after affirmative construction.[3]

Key to columns: number of occurrences followed by (1) indicative; (2) future; (3) conditional; (4) indeterminate verb form; (5) subjunctive; (6) subjunctive employed with conditional force.

	(1)	(2)	(3)	(4)	(5)	(6)
vouloir	4	—	—	98	116	—
commander	—	—	1	32	46	—
prier	7(§58)	1c	1	62	65	—
dire	—	—	—	53	64	—
faire	—	2	2	9	19	—
empêcher	1	—	—	12	12	—
permettre	—	—	—	3	13	—
trouver bon	2	—	—	6	4	—
trouver mauvais	3	—	—	4	1	—
ordonner	—	2	6	11	18	—

Causative and Related Expressions

70. Between Commynes and Malherbe usage changes as regards construction following causative verbs. The objective clause becomes less generally employed after verbs which may be followed by either an objective or a consecutive clause. The principle of the later usage is illustrated by Malherbe's statement, made in correcting Desportes, that the subjunctive mood, that is, the objective clause, may be used in the case of *faire que* only after the imperative form (Malh., IV, 262, 368). In conformity with this precept Malherbe follows the same rule in his employment of *empêcher que* (III, 11, 499). Examination of Malherbe's practice shows that he uses the subjunctive whenever volition is present, e.g.:

Dieu fasse que la fin *réponde* au commencement! (III, 166); le Roi et Monsieur le connétable ... l'*avoient prié d'empêcher* qu'elle n'*allât* en Espagne (III, 162).

In the works of earlier authors there is a somewhat freer usage of the objective clause.

[3] See Chapter I, p. 8, note 3.

IN SUBJECTIVE CLAUSES

AFTER EXPRESSIONS OF NECESSITY, VOLITION, ETC.

71. After the entire range of these expressions the subjunctive is employed in the statement or formulation of the unfulfilled condition. This manner of expressing the reason for subjunctive usage has a broad application. For example, *désirer*, which is employed as a purely volitional expression, means primarily "to be out of place" or "to be lacking," in its Latin form, *desiderare*, applied to soldiers missing from the ranks.

We may divide these introductory expressions into several groups, according to their implications:

   I. The condition is necessary, that is, lacking.
  II. The introductory expression states how much, or what, is lacking for the fulfillment of the condition.
 III. The introductory expression characterizes the fulfillment of the condition as satisfactory or sufficient, as a considerable matter, as an easy matter, etc.
 IV. The introductory expression indicates that fulfillment of the condition (1) is incumbent, (2) is made incumbent by custom, precedent, or the practice of the majority, or (3) is made incumbent by its appropriateness.
  V. The introductory expression implies that fulfillment of the condition is approved or disapproved owing to its appropriateness, inconvenience, reasonableness, unreasonableness, etc.
 VI. Fulfillment of the condition is desired or is not desired: (1) declarative expressions employed to express volition; (2) volitional expressions indicating a resolution; (3) indirect expressions of volition.
VII. The introductory expression characterizes the condition as advantageous or as disadvantageous.

Examples

   72. Group I:

il est besoin	il est nécessité
il s'ensuit	il reste
il faut	
il est nécessaire	il n'y aurait faute

parquoy *est besoing* qu'elle *prenne* quelque corps (Marg., II, 123); *il s'ensuit* que le nombre des termes . . . *soit* plus grand. (Est., 150); *il falloit* qu'il *allast* à Romme (Desp., 29); *Il faut* bien qu'il *soit* bon, puisqu'il l'est aux meschants mesme. (Mont., III, 377); *Il est necessaire* qu'ilz *soyent* icy surprins au passage. (Calv., R. C., xxxiv); *il est necessité* que chascun seigneur et prince *ayt* son contraire (Comm., II, 237); *il reste* . . . avecq ma main ie *rende* mon corps semblable au vostre (Marg., III, 209).

les asseüroit bien le roy qu'*il n'y auroit point de faulte* qu'il ne *baillast* la possession dudict pays. (Comm., I, 171); luy manda qu'*il n'y auroit poinct de faulte* qu'il ne se *trouva** à l'heure qu'elle luy mandoyt (Marg., III, 41).

It may be recalled that we have noted (§34) in the work of Gautier d'Arras an example of the periphrastic future after an expression of this type (*il estuet*) expressing the unfulfilled condition.

73. Group II:

Toutesfois *il s'en faillut bien peu* qu'ilz n'en *vinsent* à leur intencion. (Comm., I, 156); *il ne failloit que tenir encores troys jours* qu'ilz n'*eussent* eu le secours. (*id.*, II, 134); *Il ne luy fault que la parolle*, que ce ne *soit* un homme (Desp., 221); *ne s'en a guère fallu* que ses pas ne *soient* glissés (Calv., O. F., 86); *il ne s'en faut pas beaucoup* qu'il ne *soit* délaissé (*id.*, O. F., 93); Mais *tant s'en faut* que ce *soit* chose qu'il desire (Vair, 92); *Combien s'en a-il fallu* que ceste . . . Cité . . . ne *soit* demeurée captive . . .? (*id.*, 189); *il ne s'en est rien fallu* que vous n'*ayez* rien eu de moi (Malh., III, 175); *Il s'en faut beaucoup* que 66 ne *soit* bien comme de coutume (*id.*, III, 348).

In Commynes and in earlier authors we find also the indicative:

ilz l'avoient trouvé en telle collère contre le roy d'Angleterre que *à peu* qu'ilz ne l'*avoient* gaigné (Comm., II, 50); Chr., 884, 1988; Gaut., 1714 (*Petit en faut* qu'il n'*est* estainz.)

74. Group III:

il me *suffit* que vous *voyiez* que je suis votre serviteur (Malh., III, 225); *il est* beaucoup plus *facile*, où le populaire ha auctorité, qu'il *esmeuve* seditions. (Calv., R. C., 760); Encores *est ce beaucoup* que nous *puissions* couvrir noz imperfections. (Marg., III, 62); *il suffit assez* que vous *sçachiez* faire mal. (*id.*, III, 113); *C'est assez* que deux *soient* mortz d'amour (*id.*, III, 215).

In this last example the condition is a fulfilled one. In such a case, that is, one stressing factual quality, we sometimes find the indicative:

il suffit bien que un roy *employe** quelquefois son loisir à ouir chanter les chantres, et fait beaucoup d'honneur aux Muses (Amy., 2); Chr., 6007.

Some parallel cases are indicated in §32, where attention is called to the declarative usage of the expressions.

75. Group IV:

(1) *fut force* que la pluspart des gens . . . *allassent* à pied (Comm., I, 167); *il est force* qu'ilz *ayent* beaucoup veu (Amy., xi); *il est temps* que i'en *congnoisse* la verité (Marg., I, 132); puis que telle *est* ceste fatale *destinée* que par iceulx *soye* inquieté . . . (Rab., G., 29-5)

(2) *c'est chose accoustumée* (Comm., I, 3); *ce n'est de coustume* (Rab., G., 34-54); Sainct Paul tesmoigne ce *estre perpetuel* à l'Evangile (Calv., R. C., xxxix); *estant la coustume* (Amy., 106); *C'est . . . une ceremonie ordinaire* (Mont., I, 57); Gaut., 6465 (*est chascuns coustumiers*).

(3) *il appartient* (Calv., R. C., xviii); *il est convenable* (*id.*, R. C., 11); *il convient* (*id.*, R. C., 768); *il n'y a nul inconvenient* (*id.*, R. C., 768); combien qu'*il soit grandement utile* (*id.*, O. F., 32); Aussi *n'est il pas inconvenient* (Amy., 9).

76. Group V:

il seroit bien employé	il n'y a pas raison
ce seroit trop d'incommodité	il n'est pas raisonnable
il est juste	il ne semble pas raisonnable
c'est une chose juste	
c'est raison	est-il raisonnable?
il est raisonnable	y a-t-il raison?
ce n'est pas raison	n'est-ce pas raison?

ce seroit trop d'incommodité . . . que le quartier *expirât* pour les uns et *commençât* pour les autres (Malh., III, 207); *Il seroit bien employé* . . . que vous *eussiez* une telle femme (Marg., III, 78).

77. Group VI:

(1) il . . . demanda à aucuns s'*il leur sembloit* qu'ilz *attendissent* l'assault. (Comm., I, 237); *il estoit bien advis à Fabius* . . . que celuy qui prent à gouverner des hommes, *n'usast* plus de patience . . . que . . . (Amy., 99).

Devoir forms an exception:

Et *sembla à tout son conseil* que en toute force il se *doibvoit* defendre. (Rab., G., 32-26)

(2) *feut avisé* entre eulx que à cest office *seroit* mis Ponocrates . . . et que tous . . . *iroient* à Paris (Rab., G., 15-56).

This case corresponds to those in §§ 63-66. We find similar expressions employed to indicate approval, followed by the subjunctive, e.g.:

C'est bien advisé que chascun en *dye* comme il l'entend. (Fail, P. R., 45)

The subjunctive is also used after negative expressions corresponding to *ordonner* and *moyenner:*

il n'y a ordre qu'en l'humeur où je suis je vous *puisse* entretenir comme je voudrois (Malh., III, 496); *Il n'y a moyen* que je lui *écrive* (*id.*, III, 65).

But the force of this negative employment (*il est impossible*) varies somewhat from that of the affirmative:

je devois . . . mener ma besogne d'un *ordre* que le plus friand *fût* servi le dernier. (Malh., II, 214)

(3) *il plaît (à qlqn)*; *il tarde (à qlqn)*; *il ne tient pas (à qlqn).*

il ne tiendra pas à M. des Diguières que Milan ne *soit* assiégé (Malh., III, 133); mon histoire est si belle . . . qu'*il me tarde* que vous la *sachiez* comme moy. (Marg., I, 97)

After *tarder* the indicative is sometimes employed to express the cause of the sentiment or longing:

il luy tarda bien qu'elle ne le *pouvoit* reveoir (Marg., I, 242); *luy tarda bien* que le iour & heure n'*estoient* venuz. (*id.*, III, 108)

78. Group VII:

c'est grand bien	il vaut mieux (à qlqn)
il est bon (except §32)	c'est grand richesse
il importe	le plus sûr est
il n'y a point de mal	il est danger
le meilleur est	il y a danger
le mieux est	

C'est grand richesse à ung prince d'avoir en sa compaignie ung saige homme . . . et que cestuy-là *ayt* loy de luy dire vérité. (Comm., I, 205); *il y a danger* qu'il . . . ne les *faille* renvoyer ailleurs. (Malh., III, 316); *Quel danger y auroit-il* que les plus sages *vuidassent* ainsi les nostres, . . . ? (Mont., III, 381)

79. The division of the expressions above into seven groups involves perforce certain arbitrary placements, even, for example, of a single expression:

Il fault que le diable l'ayt emporté, car ie l'ay veu entrer icy (Marg., II, 207).

Faut il qu'une religieuse sçaiche qu'elle ait des tetins? (*id.*, II, 63)

The segregation of examples of indicative usage in §32 is likewise more or less arbitrary. The line of division may be discerned, however, merely by noting that the indicative does not occur after the future or the present conditional, which are assumptive moods and introduce the unfulfilled condition.

RÉSUMÉ

Volition

80. Construction after volitional expressions ranges through the purpose clause, the simple objective clause, and the consecutive clause. Wherever the latter follows a causative expression it becomes subject, at the end of the sixteenth century, to a rule which distinguishes the construction to be followed by an objective clause from the construction to be followed by a consecutive clause.

Subjunctive usage in dependent clauses is the general rule. Exceptions occur only after affirmative construction. Occasionally, after expressions of entreaty, we find a hypotactic imperative. Past tenses of the indicative occur only after such expressions as *Dieu voulut* or *mon malheur voulut*, employed with essentially declarative force, equivalent to *il arriva*.

The conditional and the future occur only after expressions indicating a resolution, a decision, or an arrangement implying a disposition as distinguished from a wish. In the latter half of the sixteenth century the employment of the future or the conditional tends to occur only after those expressions which are recognizable as belonging to the language of a governing body or final authority; not, however, to the exclusion of subjunctive usage.

Impersonal Expressions

81. The subjunctive is invariable in the expression of the unfulfilled condition; but in sentences dealing with facts the action of the

dependent clause is not invariably presented as being contingent upon the action of the impersonal expression, and the indicative is employed. Here, as in the case of clauses introduced by *que* after expressions of emotion, subjunctive usage is not solidly established.

After expressions denoting necessity, incumbency, or volition the subjunctive is invariable.

CHAPTER IV

IN ADVERBIAL CLAUSES OF PURPOSE

82. Since in the material examined there is no occurrence of the indicative, future, or conditional in adverbial clauses of purpose, we may say that the subjunctive is the rule. Even the pluperfect subjunctive, which is frequently interchangeable with the past conditional, is employed as a true subjunctive expressing an anterior contingency:

pour . . . entrer sans danger chez ma mye, j'eusse pris souvent la forme et la face de l'une de ses voisines, *à celle fin que* l'on ne m'*eust cogneu* (Desp., 325).

M. Brunot notes that the indicative [future] is still found after *afin que* at the beginning of the sixteenth century:

c'est assavoir *afin que* les sujets de nos princes *entendront* l'illustrité de leurs princes ancestres (Lem. des Belges, 5; dans Hug., *o. c.*, 201). (Brun., *Hist.*, II, 447)

The future, in fact, was still employed a century later, since there can be no other logical explanation of Oudin's correction:

Afin que i'aye: . . . ne se peut mettre avec le futur de l'indicatif, *afin que i'auray.* (Oud. 1640, 303)

83. In connection with this apparently rare use of the future in purpose clauses it is to be noted that the sense relationship between purpose clauses and consecutive clauses is very close where a conditional (past future) or a future occurs in a consecutive construction. We may take an early example as an illustration:

> Amené sont, leiier les fet
> Et dit qu'il ne seront detret,
> Tant qu'antor le chastel seront,
> *Si que* cil dedanz les *verront.*
>   (Chr., 1445)

The sense of the adjectival clause[1] likewise may approach that of the purpose clause:

de moy n'aurez auiourd'huy chose *qui vous puisse plaire.* (Marg., I, 64)

Mes enfans, vous me demandez . . . ung passetemps *qui vous puisse delivrer de vos ennuictz* (*id.*, I, 11).

afin que toujours vous ayez quelque objet *qui vous ramentoive* que . . . (Malh., III, 68).

It is evident that such comparisons could be carried to considerable length. The following one, for example, spans the constructional difference between a purpose clause and the ordinary objective clause:

l'on y pourroit mettre ordre et *que* les gens d'armes fussent payéz de deux moys en deux moys pour le plus tard. (Comm., II, 216)

il faut . . . *mettre ordre que* nous ne soyons prevenus (Vair, 138).

84. The purpose clause is generally introduced by one of the following conjunctions or conjunctive locutions:

que	par quoy
à ce que	pour que
afin que	de crainte que
à celle fin que	de peur que
à ceste fin que	dont

Monsieur le diable, descendez *que* je *aye* le roussin (Rab., G., 34-55); Et bien, Monsieur, *à ce que* rien ne *soit* trompé, marché nul, voila mon denier à Dieu (Fail, Eutr., 243); *A celle fin que* le dormir mesme ne m'*eschapat* . . ., j'ay autresfois trouvé bon qu'on me le troublat *pour que* je l'*entrevisse.* (Mont., III, 445); Le Roy . . . prouvent [prouveut] sagement qu'on n'y menast aucuns escholiers de la jurisprudence, *de crainte que* les proces ne *peuplassent* en ce nouveau monde (*id.*, III, 381); *de peur que* les gens de la justice ne les y *attrapassent* (*id.*, III, 387); il m'a semblé estre expedient, de faire servir ce present livre . . . de confession de Foy envers toy: *dont* tu *congnoisses* quelle est la doctrine, contre laquelle . . . (Calv., R. C., vi).

Par quoy has practically disappeared at the beginning of our period, although frequently found in Froissart:

---

[1] Compare: . . . pour l'amour que Diex avoit au roy, qui la poour metoit ou cuer à nos ennemis, *pour quoy* il ne nous *osassent* venir courre sus. (Joinville, *Histoire de Saint Louis* [ed. Natalis de Wailly, Paris, 1868], p. 4).

Auquns clers escripsent et registrent lors œuvres et baceleries, *par quoi* elles *soient* misses et couchies en mémores perpétuelles (Froiss., II, 13).

Its successor, *dont* ([afin que] de unde), is exceptional. *Pour que*, which is extremely rare in comparison with *afin que*, replaces *pour ce que*, which is frequent in Chrétien and occasional in Froissart:

Et *pour ce que* ou temps advenir on *sace* de vérité qui ce livre mist sus, on m'apelle sire Jehan Froissart (Froiss., II, 2).

De crainte que is exceptional in comparison with *de peur que*, which, like *à celle fin*, is not accepted by the grammarians of the following century (Oud. 1640, 300; Vaug.-Chass., II, 427).

Pour que

85. In the seventeenth century Vaugelas notes that *pour que* is much used along the Loire and that Cardinal Richelieu has helped to bring it into usage at the court (Vaug.-Chass., I, 72). Vaugelas admits its convenience, but disapproves its employment. The French Academy finally admits *assez pour que*.

It has been stated that the first example of *pour que* employed to introduce a purpose clause occurs in Gautier's *Ille et Galeron* (Ritchie, p. 61; ed. Foerster, Halle, 1891 [ed. Löseth, line 1243]). A similar example occurs in line 1225 (ed. Löseth). In both examples, however, *pour que* is employed with the sense of *pourvu que*. Further examples of *pour que* employed in this sense occur in Gaut., 386 (variant T: *pour che que*; B: *pruec ke*); 2171; 4178 (variant B: *pruec ke*); 5393 (variant T: *si*). As the variants show, there was some confusion among *pour ce que*, *pour que*, and *pro ce que* (*pourvu que*). At the same time Chrétien employs *por ce que* to express both *parce que* and *afin que:*

> Mes un an leissa eschaper
> Por ce qu'il *ierent* per a per,
> Et por ce que par lui *seüst*
> Li dus sa perte et duel *eüst.*
> (Chr., 3809)

Here the sense of the second *por ce que* is recognizable only from the mood or the context. We are forced to read: *pour ce, que.*

This *pour ce que* remains in Froissart (§84). It is doubtful whether the *pour que* used in the sixteenth century derives from it.

Pour que is not popular in the sixteenth century. This may be due to the possibility of confusion of conjunctive *que* with relative *que*, since they are destined to be followed by the same construction and mood:

Ce n'est pas un motif *pour que* le peuple *prenne* sa défense (France, 279).

Here we are dealing, historically speaking, with a relative clause modifying a negated antecedent. Compare:

Negative antecedent: mais que Dieu me pardonne & mon mary aussy il n'y a rien *pourquoy* ie *voulsisse* morir. (Marg., II, 179)

Affirmative antecedent: la dame laissa la porte entre ouverte, & alluma de la clairté dedans *pourquoy* la beaulté de ceste fille *pouvait* estre veue clairement. (*id.*, I, 240)

Ancor n'ai je *gueires* sofert, *Por quoi* tant demanter me *doive*. (Chr., 1014); chascune a *assez* en soi *Pour quoi* les *doive* refuser (Gaut., 2473); li roys fu envoyet . . . en ung chastel . . . séant sus le belle rivière de Saverne, ou *assés* priès *que* je n'en *mente* (Froiss., II, 84); le prévôt s'était éveillé . . . d'*assez* mauvaise humeur . . . *pour que* sa fureur n'*eût* pas besoin d'être attisée (V. Hugo, *Notre Dame de Paris*).

During our period the purpose clause is frequently a relative or an ajectival clause, but of clear construction, e.g.:

donne moy quelque raison qui aye apparence de verité, pour me faire croyre que ton dire soit fondé . . . (Paliss., 165); baille moi quelques raisons *par lesquelles ie puisse connoistre* qu'il y a quelque apparence de verité en ton opinion. (*id.*, 158)

Consequently, one would hesitate to derive *pour que* conjunctive from *pour quoi* relative.

It seems most probable that *pour que* results from an accident of construction, bringing together *pour* and *que*. Such accidents are not uncommon (e.g., §83, Comm., II, 216). The following series of examples, chronologically arranged, will serve as illustrations of this process:

fu ordonné . . . que on metteroit en escript tous les fès . . ., *par quoy* on les *peuist* lire . . ., *et que* li saige dou pays *peuissent* sour ce prendre bon avis et acord comment et par qui les pays seroient gouvernés de dont en avant. (Froiss., II, 96) c'estoit *pour maintenir* plus seürement leurs estatz *et que* le roy ne *brouillast* parmy eulx (Comm., I, 179); son emprise de Lorraine, qu'il desiroit fort mener à fin *pour avoir* le passaige de Luxembourg en Bourgongne *et que* toutes ses seigneuries *joignissent* ensemble (*id.*, II, 88); Et luy offroit le roy de . . . luy payer dix mil Angloys pour quatre moys, affin que plus aysée-ment il portast les mises de l'armée; et luy prestoit grand nombre d'artil-lerie, gens et charroys *pour* la *conduyre* et *pour* s'en *ayder et que* ledit roy d'Angleterre *feïst** la conqueste du pays de Flandres (*id.*, II, 248).

Baillera-t-il quelque chose à Dieu *pour* son appointement et *pour* le prix de la rançon de son âme, *et qu'*il *travaille** à jamais, et *vive* jusques à la fin? (Calv., O. F., 96)

pour ne *demeurer* courts *et que* faute d'argent ne vous *face* perdre . . . (Fail, Eutr., 262).

pour que je l'*entrevisse*. (Mont., III, 445)

If we were dealing with an earlier period of the language *pour que* would derive more readily through *por ce que—pour ce que— pource que—pour que*, dropping the atonic *ce*. Modern *pour que*, however, appears to originate in the sixteenth century.

Résumé

86. As for mood usage in the purpose clause, the subjunctive is practically invariable. Historically considered, the construction of the purpose clause, in some cases, and its sense, in other cases, bear close relation to other types of clauses, and especially to the consecutive clause and the optative clause. This, however, is merely the result of the close but supple syntax which character-izes the language.

Since the conjunctive locution offers the sole variable, we may conclude with a table of comparative frequencies:

	que	à ce que	de peur que	pour ce que	par quoy	afin que à celle or ceste fin que	pour que	de crainte que	dont
Gaut.	15	1	2	—	—	—	—	—	—
Chr.	5	—	—	23	—	—	—	—	—
Froiss.	2	—	—	3	15	26	—	—	—
Comm.	—	—	7	—	1	45	4	—	—

	que	à ce que	de peur que	pour ce que	par quoy	afin que à celle or ceste fin que	pour que	de crainte que	dont
Marg.	5	—	14	—	—	59	1	—	—
Rab.	9	3	1	—	—	37	—	—	—
Desp.	3	—	5	—	—	33	—	—	—
Calv.	1	17	8	—	—	97	2	—	2
Fail	—	3	—	—	—	9	1	—	—
Rons.	—	—	1	—	—	7	—	—	—
Paliss.	—	3	1	—	—	38	—	—	—
Amy.	—	—	5	—	—	17	—	—	—
Est.	—	—	—	—	—	14	—	—	—
Mont.	2	4	6	—	—	12	1	1	—
Vair	3	—	8	—	—	27	—	—	—
Malh.	—	—	1	—	—	21	—	—	—
France	—	—	1	—	—	6	8	—	—

The purpose clause is primarily distinguishable through mood and context. From the table it is evident that the purpose clause now becomes more readily distinguishable through the increasing employment of some conjunctive locution serving as an exclusive label, implying a specific idea, such as that of prevention (*peur*) or of causation (*fin*).

CHAPTER V

IN CONSECUTIVE CLAUSES

OF PURPOSE

87. In consecutive clauses which present the result yet to be obtained, and which are comparable to clauses of purpose, we find the subjunctive.

Manner

88. The conjunctive locutions expressing manner, employed during our period to introduce consecutive clauses of purpose, are:

en sorte que	par tel moyen que
en façon que	si que
de telle façon que	tellement que
en telle façon que	que
de manière que	

il te convient . . . estre à luy adjoinct *en sorte que* jamais n'en *soys* desamparé par peché. (Rab., P., 8-129); la prudence . . . doit estre de . . . les proportionner *en telle façon qu*'elles se *puissent* toutes deux conserver. (Vair, 60); Fabius estoit d'opinion qu'il valloit mieulx les contenir par doulx et humain traittement, *de maniere qu*'ilz *eussent* honte de se remuer sans occasion (Amy., 98); si nous voullons bien pourvoir aux consciences: *si qu*'elles ne *soient* point agitées en perpetuelle doubte, il nous fault . . . (Calv., R. C., 21); Voila que c'est de pure et vraye religion, c'est à scavoir la foy conjoincte avec crainte de Dieu non faincte, *tellement que* soubz le nom de crainte *soit* comprinse . . . la dilection de sa justice (*id.*, R. C., 9); Si Grandgousier nous mettoit siege, . . . m'en irois faire arracher les dents toutes, seulement *que* troys me *restassent*, autant, à voz gens comme à moy: avec icelles nous n'avangerons que trop à manger noz munitions. (Rab., G., 32-77)

Likewise after negation:

Il greva beaucoup au roy de dissimuler . . . ; mais . . . n'y voulut point respondre *en façon qu*'ilz *congneüssent* qu'il eust mal prins (Comm., II, 51).

Tel

89. *Tel*, pronoun or adjective, is followed by a clause fulfilling a function similar to that of the adjectival clause of characteristic or specification:

ie seray très content qu'il trouve party *tel* qu'il y *puisse* vivre selon qu'il merite. (Marg., I, 234); ie veulx faire *telle* preuve de la verité que ie n'en *puisse* iamais douter (*id.*, II, 94); Mont., III, 371.

pour moyenner que ceux qui doyvent entrer aux charges soyent *tels* qu'ils *puissent* nourrir la paix (Vair, 200).

si on cherche quelque part entre les hommes *telle* ignorance, que Dieu ne *soit* point congneu . . . (Calv., R. C., 4); Si le pays . . . est de *telle* nature que les pluyes qui tombent dessus *ayent* en elles une . . . (Paliss., 345).

C'est grand cas d'avoir peu donner *tel* ordre aux pures imaginations d'un enfant, que . . . il en *ait* produict les plus beaux effects de nostre ame. (Mont., III, 342)

Non, non, Seigneur Lupolde, vous n'estes *tel*, . . . qu'on ne se *puisse* ou *doive* se moquer de vous (Fail, Eutr., 293).

Intensity

90. The conjunctive locutions expressing intensity are less numerous:

si . . . que	tellement . . . que
tant . . . que	

Il faut . . . que le feu soit *si* grand *qu'*il *aye* puissance de faire bouillir les eaux encloses (Paliss., 150); affoiblir *tant* son corps *que* la memoire de la mort luy *soyt* pour souveraine consolation. (Marg., III, 154); Ne vault-il pas mieux en boire *tant*, *qu'*il en *sorte* par les yeux, . . .? (Desp., 202); faictes *tant* que *ayons* de l'eaue fresche (Rab., P., 18-96); Les Espagnols . . . tentent-ils de nouveaux moyens pour noüer *tellement* la querelle qu'elle *puisse* estre irreconciliable à jamais. (Vair, 121)

OF RESULT

91. In consecutive clauses of result the indicative is used to express present or past action. If the action is assumed and subsequent to that of the main verb, the conditional or the future is employed.

Manner

92. The list of conjunctive locutions expressing manner and introducing consecutive clauses of result includes practically all those used to introduce consecutive clauses of purpose:

de façon que	en sorte que
de telle façon que	en telle sorte que
en façon que	de mode que
en telle façon que	ainsi que
de manière que	si que
en manière que	si bien que
par telle manière que	tellement que
de sorte que	que
de telle sorte que	

je . . . couppe . . . l'estriviere . . ., *en sorte qu'*elle ne *tient* que à un fillet. (Rab., P., 17-126); l'on fist XVII grosses pommes de cuyvre, . . . *en telle façon qu'*on les *ouvroit* par le mylieu (*id.*, P., 33-45); Le roy . . . s'enfermoit *tellement que* peu de gens le *veoyent*. (Comm., II, 288); luy aprint sa charte *si bien qu'*il la *disoit* par cueur au rebours (Rab., G., 14-27).

il feroit *par telle manière qu'*il *seroit* bien logé (Comm., II, 56); il eut pascience et delibera de y donner ordre *en façon que* l'on n'*entreprendroit* pas telles choses sans son sceü. (*id.*, II, 277)

The non-conjunctive portion of the locution is sometimes superfluous, as in these last two examples (cf. *faire que, donner ordre que*) and in Rab., P., 18-96, §90.

We find the indicative also after interrogation:

Blasphement ilz *en ceste façon* les justes et sainctz de Dieu *qu'*ilz les *font* semblables aux diables, . . .? (Rab., G., 45-44)

Conclusive Conjunctions

93. Conclusive conjunctions appear in consecutive construction more frequently in the earlier works of our period than in the later ones. The list in §92 includes them. Examples of their employment as conclusive conjunctions:

le feist courir encontre le soleil, *si que* l'umbre tumboit par derriere (Rab., G., 14-14); un homme estoit devenu fort riche, *de sorte qu'*il acheptoit les terres de ses voisins (Desp., 152); l'abbé . . . se commença à fascher: *de mode qu'*il ne prenoit plus plaisir en rien (*id.*, 224); le Roi me fit promettre de lui donner des vers, *tellement qu'*à cette heure il ne s'y faut plus endormir. (Malh., III, 5); Notre monde n'est revenu que ce matin de ce voyage, *si bien que* je n'ai eu loisir d'en savoir rien de plus particulier. (*id.*, III, 30)

Intensity

94. Some of the conclusive conjunctions have adverbial force in the earlier works, and express intensity, as in Rab., G., 14-27, §92; and in:

Vet *einsi* ferir un gloton, *Que* ne li valut un boton Ne li escuz ne li haubers (Chr., 1775); [li rois] Qui *si* lor randra les merites, *Que* lor dessertes seront quites. (*id.*, 2157)

In our period the conjunctive locutions involve:

si	tel
tant	tellement

j'y étois logé *si* loin du château, *que* je ne *voyois* pas un . . . (Malh., III, 38); Dieu . . . *tant* luy diminua du sens, *qu'*il *mesprisoit* tout autre conseil (Comm., I, 79); J'appenderoys à ta divinité Un livre enflé de *telle* gravité, *Que* Du Bellay luy *quitteroyt* la place. (Rons., A., 66); m'ont *tellement* estonné *que* ie ne luy *ay sceu* que dire. (Marg., I, 103)

fut leur question *jusques là que* les gens . . . *furent* prestz à aller assaillir ledict duc (Comm., I, 89).

Tant que is also employed as a conclusive conjunction:

je me suis mis . . . à continuer de traduire ce qui m'en restoit: *tant que* finablement . . . j'ay pris la hardiesse de la vous presenter imprimee (Amy., III).

The subjunctive is exceptional (e.g., Mont., I, 62). As usual, it occurs in inversions:

Je suis bien aise de l'humeur que vous avez, si portée à obliger que *ce soit vous faire plaisir que vous en demander*. (Malh., III, 378)

NEGATION, INTERROGATION, CONDITION

95. Negation, interrogation, and condition in the consecutive construction are ordinarily followed by the subjunctive.

Negation

96. *Si:*

la vie des hommes *n'*a jamais esté *si* bien reiglée, que les meilleures choses *pleussent* à la plus grand'part. (Calv., R. C., xxvii); L'aspre torment *ne* m'est point *si* amer, *Qu'*il ne me *plaise* (Rons., A., 12).

The construction with double negation is very common in the early part of our period. It is employed even to the point of expressing in the subjunctive a past fact introduced by temporal *que:*

ne fust pas si-tost au lict, *que* de plain sault il ne se *ruast* dessus ce mareschal (Desp., 166); Il ne fut pas si tost entré *que* monsieur l'archediacre ne luy *commençast* à chanter . . . (*id.*, 17); Il ne luy eut si tost le dos tourné . . . *qu'*elle ne s'*escriast* . . . (Fail, Eutr., 312); les eaux n'ont pas si tost laissé lesdits trous ou canaux vuides, *qu'*ils ne *soyent* remplis d'aër (Paliss., 167).

In the latter part of our period the formula seems to have been broken in favor of a more logical mood usage after *que* employed with the force of *quand:*

mais ce mariage . . . ne fut pas si tost faict *que* plusieurs des grands du païs en *entrerent* en jalousie (Vair, 10).

The subjunctive with conditional force occurs frequently in the earlier authors, but rarely in the later ones:

elles *ne* sçauroient estre *si* meschantes *qu'*ilz ne s'en *contentassent* (Comm., II, 50); *N'*ai pas ancor *si* grant vertu, *Que* je *poïsse* armes porter. (Chr., 146); Gaut., 2222; Froiss., II, 92.

ie *n'*aurois pas *si* tost baissé la partie prochaine de la maison de deux pieds, *que* l'autre partie ne se *trouvast* plus haute de quatre pieds (Paliss., 175).

The indicative is exceptional:

nous *ne* sommes encores *si* mortiffiez *qu'*il nous *fault* quelque passetemps & exercice corporel (Marg., I, 12).

97. *Tant:*

ne pensez *tant* à mes faultes *que* ne *pensiez* bien es vostres. (Rab., P., 34-22)

Tel (rare):

Je say assez que nostre temps et vieillesse *ne* tiennent *tel* rang et reputation, *qu'*on y *puisse* faire grand fond (Fail, Eutr., 215).

Tellement:

il *n'*est pas *tellement* estonné . . ., *qu'*il s'en *veuille* substraire (Calv., R. C., 9).

Jusque-là:

Je suis . . . paresseux, mais *non pas jusque-là que* je me *souvienne* si mal de . . . (Malh., III, 562).

98. *Sans que* may be considered a negative conjunction of manner:

je rompray ce fust icy dessus les verres *sans que* les verres *soient* en rien rompus (Rab., P., 27-108).

Employed as a conclusive conjunction:

C'est assez que deux soient mortz d'amour, *sans que* l'amour en face battre deux autres (Marg., III, 215).

After negation *sans que* is frequently replaced by *que:*

l'on *n*'eust sceu . . . enlever l'image de l'ouvrier *que* toute la statue ne *fust tombée* par morceaux. . . . le Roy . . . *ne* peut sortir de sa place *sans que* tout l'Estat s'en *aille* en pieces. (Vair, 40)

Interrogation

99. Examples:

Avons nous le cueur *si* bas *que* nous *facions* noz serviteurs noz maistres (Marg., II, 263); Me *cuides tu si* ignorant *que* ie *veuille* adiouster . . .? (Paliss., 157)

Condition

100. Examples:

si les couraiges sont . . . *tellement* piquez *que* la charité en *soit* diminuée: . . . (Calv., R. C., 770); *si* l'eloquence est de *si* grande efficace, *qu*'elle *puisse* . . . (Est., 3).

The indicative and the conditional are exceptional:

si l'eloquence . . . peut quelquesfois donner *si* bien le fil aux paroles *qu*'elle les *rend* plus trenchantes . . . (Est., 3).

si la chose n'estoit de soy *tant* notoire *que* la doute en *seroit* trop plus . . . (Amy., xxi).

The modality may be transferred to a relative clause:

Si fortune vous avoyt *tant* favorisé *que* ce fut moy qui vous *portast** ceste bonne volunté, que diriez vous? (Marg., III, 187)

CAUSATIVE AND RELATED EXPRESSIONS

101. Mood usage after expressions of causative force, which has already been considered with reference to the objective clause (§70), is identical with mood usage in other consecutive clauses of

result. After the affirmative we find the indicative, future, and conditional:

il *faisoit* qu'un peu de terre . . . luy *rendoit* plus de fruict, que . . . (Paliss., 16); Cela *fut cause* que le Roy . . . et la Royne . . . *choisirent* . . . (Vair, 8); Et ce qui *fait* que nous *avons* plusieurs diminutifs . . . (Est., 98); voila qui *cause* que lesdits arbres *sont* creux (Paliss., 27).

la concurrence . . . *fait* que . . . ils ne se *soucieront* pas . . . (Vair, 127); je . . . *feray* qu'ils ne l'*auront* plus en garde. (*id.*, 187)

Ceste deesse . . . Semoit . . . qu'Astyanax . . . *feroit* Que le Troyen . . . *triompheroit* (Rons., Fr., 59); cela *causeroit* que ladite pierre se *fendroit* (Paliss., 39).

After negation or condition the subjunctive is employed:

si le duc de Saxe pouvoit *faire* avec l'Empereur qu'il lui *quittât* la possession de cet État (Malh., III, 133); *si* Dieu *faict* que nostre labeur *soit* trouvé digne (Marg., I, 15); *mais que* vous *faciez* qu'il *soit* content (Comm., I, 165).

Faire ne puis qu'Amour tousjours ne *vienne*, Parlant à moy (Rons., A., 129); le bon vouloir que j'ay vers luy, . . . *ne doit pas estre cause* que vous me *laissiez* mourir (Desp., 62).

The construction involving an expression of permission or prevention in combination with double negation is much more rarely found in the latter part of our period than in the earlier part and in the preceding authors:

à grant peine se peürent-ilz *saulver* qu'ilz *ne fussent* prins (Comm., II, 112); il *n'a* point *espargné* son propre Filz qu'il *ne* l'*ayt* livré pour nous. (Calv., R. C., xiii)

Chr., 4315, 179 (*leissier*); Gaut., 3039 (*laissier*); Chr., 2017 (*eschaper*); Froiss., XV, 268 (*celler*); XV, 299 (*apprivoisier*).

RÉSUMÉ

102. Mood usage in consecutive clauses varies according to the circumstances. Cases include the expression of purpose, with a background of volition, the expression of facts, real or assumed, inversion, and negative, interrogative, or conditioned construction. Conversely, mood is the sole index to the nature of those clauses which are introduced by conjunctive locutions of unre-

stricted employment. Occasionally a conjunctive locution merely accentuates the sense of a preceding verb which, in itself, is capable of influencing mood usage in a dependent clause.

This variety of facts leads to making certain arbitrary distinctions concerning constructions which, in some respects and employments, are identical. Thus are distinguished a purpose clause and a consecutive clause of purpose, through the conjunctive locution, and, after causative expressions, a consecutive clause and an objective clause, through the mood.

New rules are becoming distinguishable. One is perceived and indicated by Malherbe (§70). Old rules, discernible through the recurrence of certain formulas of construction constantly followed by the same mood (e.g., §96), begin to be broken. Occasionally the formation or the breaking of a rule appears to result from reason, as in the two cases noted here; but such cases are to be contrasted with the numerous unreasonable usages remaining to be decried by the grammarians of the next century.

Students and historians of the language have found the sixteenth and the two preceding centuries to be a period of promiscuous development, whereas the seventeenth begins a period of restriction and regulation. Vaugelas holds, for one thing, that the language has too many conclusive conjunctions. He accepts only three: *si bien que, de sorte que,* and *tellement que* (Vaug.-Chass., II, 160). In fact, the number of conjunctive locutions employed in consecutive construction tends to become smaller as we approach the end of the sixteenth century. In addition, two other restrictive steps are apparent in our period. First, the manipulation of conjunctive locutions, with regard to the separation of their component parts and their position in the sentence, becomes less varied. This step belongs to the sole "syntax" of Pierre de La Ramée: word order. Secondly, locutions formerly employed indiscriminately to express manner, or to express intensity, or as conclusives, tend to become restricted to a single employment. Thus the language moves towards crystallization.

CHAPTER VI

IN COMPARATIVE CLAUSES

103. Previous to our period the subjunctive in comparative clauses is not uncommon. In Froissart, in fact, the subjunctive is predominant. Various influences capable of affecting mood usage are represented in examples, e.g.:

The presence of a fact:

> Je ne cuit pas qu'il soit mains liez
> Que l'emperere *est* coureciez (Gaut., 5100).

The contingent state of the second term:

> Car plus de bonté a en soi
> Cist poulains que vostre home ont vil
> Que *n*'en *aient* li milleur mil
> Que il i aient hui veüz [supposition] (*id.*, 1546).

The negative quality of the second term:

> Mais Deus . . .
> Est mout plus forz que cil *ne soit.* (*id.*, 1221)

Compare:

> Par som le chiere qu'ele fait
> Cuide om en li *el* qu'il n'i *ait* (*id.*, 4280).

But the reasons for a variable practice are not discernible:

Plus a li poulains bñ en soi Que vous et vostre homme aves wil Que *nont* mie li milleur mil Que il i aient hui veüz (*id.*, 1546, variant T).

par quoi li royaummes et li pays fust de dont en avant mieux gouvernés que *esté n'avoit* (Froiss., II, 96); par quoi li roiaulmes et li païs fust en avant mieuls gouvernés que *esté n'euist* (*id.*, II, 98).

Hence we may assume the absence of any recognized rule governing the choice of mood.

104. In our period the subjunctive in comparative clauses is exceptional, and examples of its usage are paralleled in the same

author by others having the indicative. Let us examine a few cases of subjunctive usage:

après avoir payé des tailles trop plus grandes qu'ilz *ne deüssent*, encores ne donnent-ilz nulle ordre sur la forme de vivre de leurs gens d'armes (Comm., II, 216); Amadour estoit ung aussy honneste & vertueux chevalier qu'il en *soit* poinct (Marg., I, 147); C'est . . . ung tel que vous congnoissez autant homme de bien qu'il en *soyt* poinct (*id.*, III, 100); d'autant belle façon de visaige que i'en *aye* poinct *veu*. (*id.*, III, 128)

Compare:

le prince de Belhoste, autant honneste, vertueux, saige & beau prince qu'il y en *avoyt* poinct en la court (*id.*, III, 64).

From these comparisons of equality involving subjunctive usage, in which the second term is superlative by definition, the step to another construction is but a short one:

Vous avez aussy bon iugement que prince *qui soyt* (*id.*, III, 192).

In both cases we are dealing merely with a clause modifying an indefinite antecedent. Both of these types of construction continue to be employed:

Je me vante bien que vous verrez d'aussi bons vers que vous en *ayez* jamais *vu* de ma façon. (Malh., III, 14)

de toute autre qualité je suis aussi nonchalant et souffrant qu'*homme que j'aye cogneu* (Mont., III, 430).

105. In comparisons of inequality the subjunctive is being replaced by the indicative and the conditional, from the beginning of our period:

> Qui monte plus haut qu'il ne *doit*,
> Descend plus bas qu'il ne *voudroit*.
> (Est., 15)

The subjunctive, however, is not destined to disappear completely:

si on m'en offroit mille, ce seroit plus que je n'en *puisse* jamais avoir (Malh., III, 187); France, 325 (n'*eût* cru), cf. 310 (n'*avait* cru).

106. The formula involving *ne . . . si . . . que . . . ne*, which we have already noted as a negative-consecutive construction (§96), and which also forms a negative comparison of equality, stands as an exception to the foregoing notations, the subjunctive continuing to be used until late in our period (§96, second group of examples).

The same thing is true of the corresponding affirmative comparison of inequality:

nous souffrons *plus*tost toutes choses, *que declinions* de sa saincte parolle. (Calv., R. C., 783); Les Germains ou Allemans *plus* tost nestoyent mariés *quilz neussent presenté* la teste de leur ennemy à leur Roy. (Fail, P. R., 31); *Plus* tost sans forme ira confus le monde: *Que* je *soys* serf d'une maistresse blonde (Rons., A., 29).

plus tost fussent morts . . . *quilz neussent amassé* . . . (Fail, P. R., 48); *plus*tost creveroit de soif *que* elle *daignast* faire un pas. (*id.*, P. R., 71)

Compare:

l'heure de coucher fut *plus* tost venue *qu'*ilz *ne* s'en *apparceurent.* (Marg., II, 239); *Plu*tost *que* l'air *n'est* passé d'un oiseau. (Rons., Fr., 62); Il n'eut pas *plus* tost achevé ces paroles, *qu'*il se *leva* incontinent un grand bruit (Amy., 80).

That these formulas are comparative in construction, that one belongs to the negative-consecutive clause, and that the other belongs to the temporal clause of anteriority, is accidental. It is probably also accidental that the decline of subjunctive usage with them corresponds to a decline in the employment of *que* with the force of *avant que* and to an increase in its employment with the force of *quand*. Both employments are common in Commynes:

Nous n'eusmes point faict demye journée *que* nous *rencontrasmes* ung messaigé (Comm., II, 162); le roy de Portugal n'eut pas faict une journée, . . . *que* ledict duc de Lorraine et les Allemans . . . *ne deslogeassent* de Sainct-Nycolas (*id.*, II, 149).

Or, the last example may be read as a consecutive construction (*v.* §98), in which the formula *ne . . . que . . . ne . . . subjunctive* most frequently occurs.

Résumé

107. Mood usage in comparative clauses is already variable, or erratic, previous to our period. During it the employment of the subjunctive decreases greatly.

In comparisons of inequality, although the subjunctive is not to disappear from usage, it is being replaced by other forms, from the beginning of our period, and becomes so exceptional that its occurrence may be described as negligible.

In comparisons of equality the subjunctive persists during our period. Like the subjunctive employed in adjectival clauses modifying superlative antecedents, it is attributable to the indefiniteness of the antecedent, either apparent or hypothetical, evoked in comparison.

108. Certain formulas of construction, followed ordinarily by the same mood, occur in connection with several types of clauses. A change in mood depends on a change in the formula, if not in the sense. For example, the formula *ne . . . sitôt . . . que . . . ne . . . subjunctive* tends to be replaced by the formula *ne . . . sitôt . . . que . . . indicative*, breaking its relationship with the negative-consecutive construction as *que* becomes identified with *quand*. These points may be illustrated by three groups of examples:

(1) Negative-consecutive construction: *Non* qu'elle fust *si* supersticieuse *qu'*elle *pensast** que . . . (Marg., I, 3); nous *ne* sommes pas *si* malheureux en ceste compaignie *que* nul de tous les mariez *ne soyt* de ce nombre là. (*id.*, II, 239)

Indicative exceptional: nous *ne* sommes encores *si* mortiffiez qu'il nous *fault* quelque passetemps . . . (*id.*, I, 12).

(2) *ne . . . sitôt . . . que . . . ne . . . subjunctive:* Mais il *ne* peut *si tost* faire despecher sa lettre à la chancellerie *que* le duc & la duchesse *ne fussent* . . . advertiz (*id.*, I, 28); *si tost ne* peurent gaigner le hault *qu'*ilz *ne rencontrassent* . . . Picrochole (Rab., G., 48-40).

Compare: on *n'*a sceu *si* bien faire *que* cette assemblée *ne* se *soit* faite. (Vair, 117)

ne . . . sitôt . . . que . . . indicative: ce mariage . . . *ne* fut pas *si* tost faict *que* plusieurs des grands du païs en *entrerent* en jalousie (*id.*, 10).

(3) Formula employed inadvertently, failing to express what was intended: Panurge *n'*eut pas achevé ce mot *que* tous les chiens qui estoient en l'esglise *ne* s'en *vinssent* à ceste dame (Rab., P., 22-43, variants A, G).

Correction in a later edition gives *que* the sense of *quand:* Panurge *n'*eut achevé ce mot *que* tous les chiens qui estoient en l'eglise *acoururent* à ceste dame (*id.*, P., 22-43).

The error in the third group appears to result from analogy of construction, while the changes attending its correction attest the author's conscious restriction of the employment of the negative-consecutive formula from the sphere of the temporal clause.

CHAPTER VII

IN TEMPORAL ADVERBIAL CLAUSES

Posteriority

109. The subjunctive does not occur. *Après que, attendre après que, puis que, depuis que, sitôt que,* etc., are followed by other forms.

Simultaneity

110. *Ainsi comme, ainsi que, cependant que, pendant que, quand, que (quand), tandis que, tandis que (tant que),* and *tant que,* in connection with past time, are followed by the indicative, future, or conditional.

The subjunctive is exceptional. It occurs after *tant comme* (duration) in connection with present or future time in Chrétien (e.g., 5522, 5672), after *tant que* (duration) in connection with past time in Froissart (e.g., XV, 202), and in connection with present or future time in Froissart (e.g., XV, 300) and in Ronsard:

> Son lustre encor ne m'a point assouvy,
> Ny ne fera, non, non, *tant que* je *vive.*
> (Rons., A., 71)

It occurs after *comme* in Commynes and, without exception, in *Amyot:*

comme tous *eussent soupé* et *qu'*il y *avoit* largement gens se pourmenans par les rues, mons^r Charles de France et mons^r de Charroloys estoi[en]t à une fenestre et parloient eulx deux de très grand affection. (Comm., I, 41); Auquel *comme* Guillot *eust** envoyé son filz . . . le remercier . . ., respondit: . . . (Fail, P. R., 145).

Comme donques Archidamus . . . luy *demandast* un jour lequel luctoit le mieulx de luy ou de Pericles, il luy respondit: . . . (Amy., 13).

After *tant comme* and *tant que,* however, in both these and our other authors, the future predominates:

> Cela s'est tousjours fait, et tousjours se fera,
> *Tant que* le monde entier en ses membres *sera.* (Rons., Fr., 39)

After *mais que*, which Vaugelas says may not be written for *quand* in good style (Vaug., 162), the subjunctive is invariably used:

C'est bien; *mais que* je *sois* grand, je vous en rendrai bon compte. (Malh., III, 460); *id.*, III, 56; Marg., I, 250; Froiss., II, 21; Gaut., 6056.

Negation

111. After *sans que*, negating the simultaneity of two actions, the subjunctive is invariably found:

L'anpererriz *sanz* mal *qu'*ele *et* Se plaint et malade se fet (Chr., 5699).

Nus n'i parole *sanz* conduit *Et qu'*il *n'*i *ait* trois d'eus al mains (Gaut., 3439).

Ceulx de Gand les avoyent en grant hayne, *sans* nulle offence *qu'*ilz leur en *eussent faicte*, mais seulement pour la grant auctorité où ilz les avoyent veüz. (Comm., II, 199)

estoient ceulx de dedans tout à descouvert sur la muraille *sans que* on leur *tirast*. (*id.*, I, 228)

cela dura assez long temps, *sans que* les peres ni meres, y *missent* aucune police. (Paliss., 112)

The first and third examples above illustrate the persistency of the relative clause in construction, and the third, in addition, is equivalent to a negated causative clause. The second example may recall what was noted in §98 concerning *que . . . ne* replacing *sans que* after negation. It may also recall the derivation of *pour que* from *pour . . . et que* (§85), when compared with the fourth example. The fifth example illustrates the negation of simultaneity.

Anteriority

112. Conjunctive locutions expressing anteriority may be divided into three groups. To the first belong:

ains que	paravant que
auparavant que	plustost que
avant que	plus tost que
davant que	premier que
devant que	

After these locutions the subjunctive is the general usage. The indicative is exceptional both (1) in authors before our period and (2) in the early authors of our period:

(1) Nus ne set home que il vaut *Devant qu*'il *est* levez en haut (Gaut., 2014); *avant que* li Hainnuier *issirent* de Londres, il furent payet (Froiss., II, 95).

(2) son pauvre mary . . . veid *premier* le corps de sa femme mort devant sa maison, *qu*'il n'en *avoit sceu* les nouvelles (Marg., I, 37) (With *premier . . . que* compare *sans . . . que, pour . . . et que*, §111).

Ains and *plus tost* are occasionally employed with the sense of *plutôt*, but *ains que* and *plus tost que* (or *plustost que*) are also employed with the sense of *avant que*, followed by the subjunctive:

O Jupiter, . . . ne permets que je meure, *Ains qu*'il se *face* en armes un grand roy (Rons., Fr., 75); celluy qui ayme . . . laissera *plus tost* son ame par la mort *que* ceste forte amour *saille* de son cueur. (Marg., I, 85)

Compare:

vous devez fuir ce feu qui a *plus tost* bruslé un cueur *qu*'il *ne* s'en *est* apparceu. (*id.*, I, 198); *v.* §106, compared examples.

As examples show, at the beginning of our period there is some confusion of temporal with comparative construction. Palsgrave, however, distinguishes *avant . . . que*, "rather . . . than," from *avant que*, "byfore":

jayme *avant* mourir *que* vous offencer; *avant que* soyt jour.

And likewise in the earlier authors:

je me lairoie *ainz* ocire *Que* li desisse me destrece. (Gaut., 3793); Mout li covandroit loing aler, *Ainz qu*'il trouvast si delitable. (Chr., 5634)

113. To the second group belong:

attendre quand	que
jusques que	attendre que
jusques à l'heure que	tant que
jusques au jour que	jusqu'à tant que
à quand	jusqu'à ce que

Those of the first column are followed, in the occurrences recorded, by the indicative or the conditional. Those of the second column require a more detailed consideration.

Que is followed by the subjunctive:

Et les prieray avoir patience *qu*'ils *soyent venus* au lieu où . . . (Est., 29).

Attendre que is followed by the conditional, the future, or the subjunctive, which is predominant:

*attendant qu'*il *yroit* chercher de l'herbe . . . (Rab., P., 15-74); En *attendant que* les mers . . . *Repousseront* . . . (Rons., Fr., 108); j'*attendois* à vous écrire *que* nous *vissions* la fin de nos cérémonies (Malh., III, 177).

When negative, it is followed by the subjunctive:

ilz *n'attendoyent* point *que* les choses *fussent* perdues pour les trouver (Desp., 215).

Tant que in connection with past time is followed by the indicative in our period, although the imperfect subjunctive (equivalent to the conditional) is employed by Gautier and Chrétien.

tant que tout *alla* si mal, qu'en fin tout se trouva bien. (Fail, Eutr., 283)

Also with a consecutive sense:

tant allèrent *qu'*ilz *entrèrent* dedans ung grant boullevart (Comm., I, 83); se retira *tant* de temps *que* le bruict *cessa* . . . (Marg., I, 89).

In connection with present time we find the subjunctive:

il ne faut pas se garder *tant qu'*on *soit* usé (Desp., 58); Fais à mon Loyr ses mines relascher, *Tant que* Madame à rive *soit sortie*. (Rons., A., 166)

More rarely the future is used (Marg., I, 142).

Jusqu'à ce que and *jusqu'à tant que* in connection with past time are followed by either the indicative or the subjunctive, but the subjunctive tends to predominate after 1550:

Ceste chasse estoit sans cesse et logé par les villaiges, *jusques à ce qu'*il *venoit* quelques nouvelles de la guerre (Comm., II, 326); Mais jamais je n'ay congneu prince qui ait sceu congnoistre la difference entre les hommes, *jusques à ce qu'*il *se soit trouvé* en necessité (*id.*, I, 78).

il n'a bougé de dessus ma table que *jusques à ce que* je l'*ai mis* dans ce paquet. (Malh., III, 110)

In connection with present or future time the subjunctive and, more rarely, the future, are employed:

elle ne cessera jamais de changer . . . *jusques à ce que* . . . ses souhaits *seront* à un coup assouvis. (Amy., xvii); je ordonne . . . que Ponocrates . . . *jusques à ce qu'*il le *congnoistra* . . . (Rab., G., 50-76).

Je n'écrirai point à M. du Périer *jusques à ce que* j'*aye parlé* à lui (Malh., III, 8).

114. In the third group stands *que . . . ne,* which belongs to both the first and the second groups. Its employment is a source of confusion, as we have noted by examples in §§106, 108. Here we refer to its employment with the sense of *avant que* or of *jusqu'à ce que,* followed, in either case, by the subjunctive:

ilz ne le peurent oncques atteindre, *qu'ilz ne fussent* à Narbonne. (Desp., 121); vous n'y viendrez *qu'il ne soyt* deux heures après minuict (Marg., II, 80); Or je ne t'abandonneray jamais, *que* tu *ne* le me *ayes enseigné.* (Desp., 317); Je ne saurai autre chose de cette affaire *que* je *n'aille* au Louvre, et je ne suis pas résolu d'y aller *que* je *n'aye fait* les vers (Malh., III, 144).

Compare:

Nous en ocirions *avant* un demi-cent, tous l'un apriès l'autre, *que* nous *n'euissions* un roi à nostre séance et volenté. (Froiss., II, 91)

Que . . . ne, as we have had occasion to note previously, is employed with some flexibility of sense. The flexibility of mood usage after it is not so great. It is generally followed by the subjunctive when it is preceded by negation.

Résumé

115. The chief notations to be made concerning mood usage after these conjunctive expressions may be based on observation of usage after two of them: *avant que* (time) and *jusqu'à ce que* (duration).

Avant que, and even *avant le temps que* (Comm., I, 3: *je veinse*), during our period, is followed by the subjunctive; whereas in Froissart *avant que* introducing a past fact is occasionally followed by the indicative.

Jusqu'à ce que introducing a past fact is ordinarily followed by the indicative, but the subjunctive also occurs. *Jusqu'à ce que* introducing anticipated action is ordinarily followed by the subjunctive, but the conditional also occurs, after past tenses of the main verb, and the future, after the present tense of the main verb. In Palissy we find an indifferent usage:

les eaux qui sont tombees . . . petit à petit descendent *iusques à ce qu'*elles *ayent trouvé* la terre foncée de quelque chose (178); des eaux . . ., qui ayans percé a travers des terres, *iusques à ce qu*'elles *ont trouvé* quelque rocher pour s'arrester (349); i.e., *ayent trouvé*, in both examples.

At the close of our period the subjunctive is still employed in the case of the past fact:

devant la réception de votre lettre . . ., nous avions la malheureuse nouvelle . . ., mais on différoit de la croire, *jusques à ce que* vous l'*eussiez écrite*. Pour moi, . . . je la crus tout aussitôt qu'elle me fut dite. (Malh., III, 553)

In our period mood usage in connection with posteriority and simultaneity is well established, and mood usage in connection with anteriority is erratic.

CHAPTER VIII

IN CAUSATIVE ADVERBIAL CLAUSES

Affirmative

116. In this category the subjunctive is employed after *comme*, but tends to be displaced by the indicative in authors later than Amyot. The conditional is also employed.

Ces choses . . . ne donnent point couraige aux Princes de faire despence . . . (*comme* certes il n'*est* pas mestier de augmenter leurs cupiditez . . .) mais, *comme* il *soit* bien necessaire qu'ilz n'entreprennent rien sinon . . ., . . . il est expedient qu'ilz . . . (Calv., R. C., 765); *comme* je ne *voudrois* user des deux autres, . . . (Est., 201).

Subjunctive usage after *comme* employed in either a causative or a temporal sense extends beyond our period. Vaugelas approves Malherbe's employment of it, because he considers it more elegant than the indicative (Vaug.-Chass., II, 428), but he condemns *comme ainsi soit* (Vaug., 470).

Comme ainsi soit, in fact, has practically disappeared at the end of our period. In Calvin it occurs frequently, but in Palissy, Amyot, and Estienne its frequency steadily declines. After it the subjunctive is predominant in Calvin, and the indicative in Amyot.

Mais *comme ainsi soit, que* plusieurs choses *ayent esté* escriptes sagement . . . (Calv., R. C., xxi); Mais *comme ainsi soit que* toutes nations . . . ne *sont* pas propres à . . . (Amy., ii).

Compare:

Puis que ainsi est, qu'avons constitué deux regimes en l'homme (Calv., R. C., 753).

117. We find only the indicative, conditional, or subjunctive with conditional force after other conjunctions in this category:

car   joint que
consideré que   mêmement que
attendu que   à cause que

90

parce que	entant que
pource que	pourtant que
pour cause que	par autant que
à raison que	pour autant que
puisque	vu que
d'autant que	

Et *pour ce que* je ne *vouldroye* point mentir (Comm., I, 2); Or, *pour ce que* je *sais* qu'il y a . . . (Calv., O. F., 28); *veu que* sans icelle, jamais l'Eglise n'*eust esté*. (*id.*, R. C., 20)

Negative

118. In the preceding pages we have frequently noted the effect of negation upon mood usage. Here again we find the subjunctive employed, after:

non que	non pour ce que
non pas que	non point d'autant que

non que la science ne *soit* aussi vraye qu'elle fut oncq, mais . . . (Desp., 50); *non pas que* je *vueille* dire que . . . (Comm., II, 165); les Romains . . . contribuerent à ses funerailles . . ., *non pource qu'*il *eust** faulte de biens pour se faire inhumer, mais seulement pour honorer sa memoire . . . (Amy., 110); Gaut., 5300 (*Non pour çou que* cil del comun Ne s'*acordassent* bien a un); Qu'ils répondent s'ils veulent qu'il a abondé, *n'ont point* [*non point*] *d'autant qu'*il *ait donné* vie plus abondante, mais pource qu'il a effacé plusieurs péchés (Calv., O. F., 70).

The same distinction between mood usage after negative construction and mood usage after affirmative construction is found in elliptical construction:

La difficulté *n'est pas que* nos filles ne *veuillent* bien aller en Espagne, mais *c'est qu'*il *faut* que . . . (Malh., III, 510).

This hybrid construction is related to the negated causative construction *ce n'est pas que* employed with the force of *ce n'est pas parce que*, distinguished from the declarative expression in §37, e.g.:

Ce n'est pas, Messieurs, *qu'*entre les deputez il n'y *ait* beaucoup de gens d'honneur (Vair, 124); §37, (1); §48, first example in second group.

We find the subjunctive also following negation:

je *ne* sais si *c'est qu'*à la vérité il le *soit* (Malh., III, 351).

Interrogative or Conditioned

119. Here, as in the case of negation, the subjunctive is employed:

Or seroit il bien malaisé de rendre la raison . . ., *si ce n'est que* lon *vueille* exalter la puissance du nombre ternaire (Amy., 71).

Seroit-ce que la hardiesse luy *fut** si commune que, pour ne l'admirer point, il la respectast moins? *Ou qu*'il l'*estimast* si proprement sienne qu'en cette hauteur il ne peust souffrir de la veoir en un autre . . .? (Mont., I, 9)

In such examples the context alone distinguishes a causative employment from an employment as a conditional conjunction, which is not invariably followed by the subjunctive:

si ce n'étoit qu'il ne *pouvoit* faire abattre celles de M. de Nevers sans abattre celles du Roi, il l'auroit fait (Malh., III, 377); les causes en sont cachées, *si ce n'est qu*'on les *apprenne* par doctrine. (Calv., O. F., 111)

Résumé

120. After the affirmative conjunctions, except *comme*, the subjunctive is not employed. After *comme* subjunctive usage persists in our period, but declines during the latter part of it.

After the negative conjunctions the subjunctive is invariable. It should be noted that these conjunctions, as well as negative constructions serving as conjunctive locutions, become affirmative in sense and are concessive, when they are followed by negation.

After negative, interrogative, and conditioned constructions serving as causative conjunctive locutions the subjunctive is employed. Consequently we may say that the subjunctive in causative clauses is traceable to negation, interrogation, condition, or *comme*.

CHAPTER IX

IN ADVERBIAL CLAUSES OF CONCESSION

Principal Conjunctions

121. The principal concessive conjunctions employed during our period are *combien que*, *bien que*, *encore que*, *nonobstant que*, and *quoique* or *quoy que*. The following table, showing their relative frequencies, indicates comparatively the rise or wane of each usage.

	nonobstant	*quoi*	*combien*	*bien*	*encore,*
Froiss.	4	21	4	—	—
Comm.	21	—	72	—	9
Marg.	13	—	120	—	20
Rab.	1	3	9	—	11
Desp.	1	1	21	—	17
Calv.	—	—	89	—	10
Fail	—	—	6	—	5
Rons.	—	1	—	10	2
Paliss.	—	—	54	—	2
Amy.	—	4	13	—	18
Est.	—	—	9	—	38
Mont.	—	6	—	1	2
Vair	1	—	4	16	1
Malh.	—	3	4	1	11
France	—	2	—	15	—

Quand, which is sometimes employed as a conditional conjunction, and much more often to introduce a concessive protasis, also occurs very frequently.[1] Of less frequent occurrence are *ja, jaçoit que, néanmoins que*, and *toutefois que*.

122. Several of our authors employ both the indicative and the subjunctive after concessive conjunctions, e.g.:

Je leur respondoye . . . que le roy Edouard estoit mort . . ., *nonobstant que* je *sçavoye* bien le contraire (Comm., I, 209); les dessusdictz chancellier et

---

[1] Modal syntax after *quand* is treated under the heading of the conditional sentence under the title mentioned in the Introduction, note 3.

seigneur . . . furent prins par lesditz Gantois, *nonobstant qu'*ilz *eussent* assez advertissemens (*id.*, II, 199).

*Encores qu'*ilz *vinsent* avecques commissions rigoreuses, si les despeschoit-il avec si bonnes parolles . . . que . . . (Comm., II, 242); *encores qu'*il *congnoissoit* clérement qu'ilz estoient comme inutilles (*id.*, II, 29); *encore que* je *crois* bien que nous y serons dans un mois, vous me manderez le prix (Malh., III, 7); M. de Soubise . . . la tient en alarme, *encore que* je *croye* que personne ne pense à une recherche si violente. (*id.*, III, 140)

Nonobstant toutes ces choses, Dieu favorisa si bien nostre affaire, que *combien que* nos assemblees *fussent* le plus souvent à plein minuit, *et que* nos ennemis nous *entendoyent* souvent passer par la ruë, si est-ce que Dieu leur tenoit la bride serree (Paliss., 109).

The usage with *combien que* represents the tendency of the century more exactly, in all its aspects, than does the usage with any other single locution. After *combien que* the subjunctive becomes decidedly predominant during the second half of the century, although there is still an indifferent mood usage in Palissy. Let us examine its mood frequency table:

Key to columns: number of occurrences followed by (1) indicative; (2) future; (3) conditional; (4) indeterminate verb form; (5) subjunctive; (6) subjunctive employed with conditional force.

combien que[2]	(1)	(2)	(3)	(4)	(5)	(6)
Froiss.	—	—	—	—	4-	—
Comm.	23–7	—	–1	26	10–4	1–
Marg.	15–4	—	–1	69	11–19	1–
Rab.	—	—	—	3	4–2	—
Desp.	1–	—	—	12	4–4	—
Calv. O. F.	1–6	—	–1	7	3–24	—
R. C.	–2	1	—	14	10–21	—
Fail	—	—	–1	3	1–1	—
Paliss.	6–1	1	–1	16	13–16	—
Amy.	—	—	—	7	3–3	—
Est.	—	—	–1	2	4–2	—
Vair	—	—	—	1	1–2	—
Malh.	–1	—	—	1	1–1	—

[2] 23-7, for example, signifies 23 occurrences in a past tense and 7 in the present tense of the mood indicated.

After *bien que*, which is the logical successor of *combien que*, but which does not displace it during our period, the ascendancy of the subjunctive is still more noticeable:

bien que	(1)	(2)	(3)	(4)	(5)	(6)
Rons.	1	—	—	2	7	—
Mont.	—	—	—	1	—	—
Vair	—	—	—	3	13	—
Malh.	—	—	—	—	1	—
France	—	—	—	—	15	—

From a comparison of these two cases it is evident that in the second half of the century we have what is practically a new mood usage after a new conjunction. That is, practice in connection with *bien que* does not appear to be affected by the tradition of indicative or erratic usage which weighs upon *combien que*. In a degree this is comparable to the cases of *cuider* and *croire*.

Real and Supposed Concession

123. Tradition is not the sole factor to be considered in examining mood usage in the concessive clause. We must also distinguish real from supposed concession, or attempt to do so, since it is not invariably possible.

The clause of real concession presents a fact in a manner to negate its factual or effective quality in a particular juncture. As we have frequently had occasion to note, there is, in our period, a strong general tendency to express facts in the indicative, regardless of syntactical analogies, whereas, on the other hand, adverbial, implied, or inherent negation tends to cause subjunctive usage. Consequently we may imagine two opposed forces as being operative in the determination of the mood of the clause of real concession, although not in the clause of supposed concession, which is closely related to the conditional clause.

Indicative usage after the concessive conjunctions could be explained by considering them to be merely adversative conjunctions whenever they are followed by the indicative, and by considering concession to be founded on, and distinguished through, subjunctive usage. The first consideration, however, would be an arbitrary one, leading to the difficulty of explaining indifferent mood usage after these conjunctions. The second, on the other hand, is very nearly in accord with the facts; for, on examining the entire body of concessive construction, without limiting our examination to usage after the principal conjunctions, we find the subjunctive to be the primary and predominant usage. But let us examine the distinction between real and supposed concession which appears to exist at the end of our period.

M. Brunot, in *La Pensée et la langue*, seems to base a theory of the concessive clause on Malherbe's correction of Desportes:

> *Bien qu'*enfin vous *fussiez* le triomphe des Dieux,
> Votre orgueilleux desir cessa quand et la vie.

"*Fussiez* est mal pour *fûtes*," says Malherbe. "*Fussiez* s'entend d'une chose douteuse; *fûtes*, d'une certaine" (Malh., IV, 319). M. Brunot takes Malherbe at his word, which is just. However, this correction of Malherbe's actually results from the fact that Desportes' verse may be read as the expression of a supposed concession (equivalent to *quand bien vous seriez*) making no sense, and not from the fact that Malherbe insists on the indicative for the expression of "things that are certain"; because, from his own work, it is evident that he does not:

On tient qu'alors cette affaire éclatera, *bien que* la Reine *ait dit* qu'elle ne veut point que Mlle de Vendôme soit mariée que le Roi n'ait dix-huit ou vingt ans. (Malh., III, 357); A quoi Mme de Nevers répondit; mais ce fut si bas que, *encore que* je *fusse* tout joignant, et que je *tendisse* l'oreille fort attentivement, je n'en pus rien ouïr, ni de ce que la Reine lui répliqua, hormis le dernier mot de la Reine, qui fut: . . . (*id.*, III, 475). Note also his indifference: *encore qu'*elle se *jeta* à genoux pour la retenir. (*id.*, III, 446)

Consequently it is evident that Malherbe makes an unconscious distinction between real and supposed concession, which Desportes does not. Between this unconscious distinction of real concession, which may be considered the only true concession, from supposed concession, which belongs properly to a protasis, and erratic or indifferent mood usage in the clause of real concession, the tendencies of mood usage during the century are encompassed and developed. Or, to express it differently, these tendencies are under the influence of traditional usage, "things that are certain," and a sense relationship to the conditional protasis. It is the traditional usage in the main body of concessive construction that will ultimately exert the determining influence on mood usage after the concessive conjunctions.

Quand

124. The concessive clause expressing either a real or a supposed concession is closely related to the conditional clause. Both, for example, employ *si:*

Real: *si* de l'estre paternel son origine *est* grande et honorable, elle n'a pas receu moins d'honneur du costé de sa mere (Vair, 5); Amy., xv; Gaut., 3909.

Supposed: *Si* nous n'en *trouvons* point, au-moins serons-nous aucunement contens de l'avoir recerché (Vair, 65); *S'il est* serjanz, la cope avra, Par cui li chastiaus pris sera. (Chr., 1547)

Both are related to the causative clause in that all three employ *quand* (e.g., causative with indicative, Chr., 1361; with subjunctive, Froiss., II, 129). The conditional and concessive employments of *quand* concur in Commynes:

Conditional: *quant* cecy ne *fust* advenu*, tout tant qu'il y avoit là de seigneurs s'en fussent tous alléz honteusement. (Comm., I, 82); *id.,* I, 70.

Concessive: *Quant* ilz *eussent eu* mil hommes d'armes avec eulx de bonne estoffe, si estoit leur entreprinse bien grande. (*id.,* I, 155); ne sçay si je l'ay dit ailleurs, et *quant* je l'*auroye dit*, si vault-il bien de dire deux foiz (*id.,* I, 250); Je . . . disoye aussi que, *quant* il ne le [mort] *seroit*, si estoient les alliances . . . telles, qu'elles ne se povoient enfraindre pour ce qui estoit advenu (*id.,* I, 209).

Throughout our period *quand* stands next to *si* in frequency of employment to introduce a protasis. From the opening of our period, however, the conditional employment of *quand* declines in favor of the concessive employment. In both employments *quand* is followed ordinarily by the pluperfect subjunctive, the past conditional, or the present conditional. In contrast with the conditional employment of *quand* in Commynes later authors begin to emphasize its concessive employment by adding *bien* or *encore*. We find *quand encore* in Amyot. Des Périers employs *quand bien* to some extent, and Henri Estienne employs it constantly.

Ce discours de raison naturelle, Sire, *quand encore* le commandement des Escritures sainctes . . . n'y *seroit* point, oblige assez tous voz subjects à desirer de vous faire service (Amy., III).

laquelle [reputation] les courtisans ne peuvent pas bonnement desguiser, *quand bien* ilz *voudroyent*. (Desp., 145); Est., 191: *eussent dict*; 21: *seroit*; 113: *aurois monstré*; 33: *serons*.

Quand encore is exceptional and *quand bien* is comparatively rare, but *quand* alone, after these compounds have come into usage, is generally concessive and is the conjunction ordinarily employed to introduce a supposed concession. The clause of supposed concession, it may be added, belongs more truly to the conditional sentence, in the matter of mood usage, than it does to general concessive construction, which is distinguished by a preponderantly subjunctive usage. *Quand* has, however, a truly conditional counterpart which stands next to it in frequency of employment in the conditional sentence. This is *qui*, which is also frequently followed by the present conditional.

Except after *quand* and its compounds, the conditional is exceptional in the concessive clause:

Et *encores que* par celles [histoires] . . . vous *pourriez* penser que . . . (Marg., II, 244); Mais, *neantmoins que* cecy *demanderoit* plus ample discours que les aureilles dun delicat (possible) souhaitteroyent, toutesfois pour ce que ce nest le principal negoce, j'ay induit ce peu, pour monstrer . . . (Fail, P. R., 34): interpreted by M. Boulenger as *vu que*, but erroneously if we compare Fail, P. R., 74, 84, 100, 108, 127, 150 (*neantmoins que*); 85 (*veu que*). Froiss., II, 136; XV, 188.

car *que* ie ne *pourrois* avoir de vous que les oz, si les voudrois ie tenir auprès de moy. (Marg., I, 138)

Remaining Cases

125. Except in the cases already noted there are practically no exceptions to subjunctive usage in the expression of concession. The remaining cases include supposed concession, alternative construction, construction involving a relative clause, and miscellaneous locutions.

Supposed Concession

Comm.: me manda que je passasse oultre, et me *deüssent*-ilz prendre, car il me rachetteroit. (I, 208); I, 237, variant B.

Marg.: quant vous auriez ceste opinion *fusse* [fût-ce] de moy mesmes, ie ne vous en donne poinct de tort (III, 21).

Rab.: ne crains . . . cheval, tant soit legier et *feust** ce Pegase de Perseus (P., 24-116); ne ausoient seulement tousser, voire *eussent ilz mangé* quinze livres de plume (P., 18-142); je accepte voluntiers l'offre, protestant jamais ne vous laisser, et *alissiez* vous à tous les diables (P., 9-152).

Fail: disoyent quilz n'oseroyent toussir . . ., *eussent ilz mangé* un plein sac de plume (P. R., 115); je combattray, &*fust* le Turc (P. R., 82).

Malh.: J'avois dit qu'il n'y avoit rien de changé; mais si a; et ne *fût*-ce que cela. (III, 174)

Alternative Construction

. . . louer toutes leurs œuvres, soient bonnes ou mauvaises. (Comm., I, 129); Soit homme ou dieu, j'embrasse tes genous. (Rons., Fr., 105); fust* bon Latin ou mauvais. (Est., 199)

il luy est . . . force de considerer . . . tout ce qui se presente à luy, utile ou inutile qu'il soit (Amy., 1).

fust* ou par ambition, ou par obstination (Amy., 107).

Soit par gosserie, soit à certes, que . . . (Mont., III, 440).

soit . . ., Ou soit . . . (Rons., Fr., 38): *ou*, being redundant before *soit*, will bring an objection from Vaugelas (Vaug.-Chass., I, 91).

Ou fust* sur le trepied, ou fust* lors qu'ils chantoient (Rons., Fr., 38). Compare Oudin: ie dirois *ou que ce fust* . . ., *ou que ce fust* . . . (Oud., 1640, 300).

Soit que nous vivions, nous vivons au Seigneur; soit que nous mourions, nous mourons au Seigneur. (Calv., O. F., 59)

Soit que je vienne en terre, ou que je retourne aux cieulx (Desp., 335); soit que le Roi pensât à cet avis, ou autrement, il pria Dieu extraordinairement (Malh., III, 167).

Miscellaneous

comment	quelque . . . qui
comment que	quelque . . . dont
	quelconque . . . qui
quelque . . . que	pour . . . que

pour . . . qui	qui que
si . . . que	quiconque
pour si peu . . . que	
tant . . . que	quoi que
tant . . .	. . . qui
. . . que	quel que
	où que
qui	. . . que

c'estoit tout un *comment* ilz *feussent* faictz participans . . . (Calv., R. C., 17); *comment que* ce *soit* que la congnoissance de Dieu et la congnoissance de nous soyent ensemble mutuellement conjoinctes: . . . (*id.*, R. C., 3).

les hommes *quelque* hardis *qu'*ilz *soient* craingnent . . . (Marg., III, 97); les hommes, *quelque* beau visage *que* fortune leur *face*, . . . (Mont., I, 96); *quelque* chose *que sachent* deliberer les hommes . . . (Comm., I, 182); *quelques* menaces et promesses *qu'*on lui *fasse*. (Malh., III, 25); *quelques* deguisemens et feintises *dont* vostre Alcibiades, Theramenes, Ulysses, et Cicero *ayent usé*, . . . (Fail, Eutr., 221); en *quelque* ville *qu'*il le *trouvast* (Comm., I, 183); en *quelque* part *que* je *sois* (Malh., III, 38); *quelque* malheur *qui* m'*ait* jamais *menacé* (Fail, Eutr., 240).

celle [puissance] *qui* . . . est bien plus grande et plus souveraine que *quelconque* autre legitime *qui puisse* estre. (Vair, 94)

n'estimant . . . *qu'*on se puisse fier du bien qui est encore en esperance de recepte, *pour* claire *qu'*elle *soit*. (Mont., I, 78); *pour* excuse *qu'*en *sceüst** faire . . ., les Angloys ne l'en vouloient croyre. (Comm., I, 224); je ne puis engraisser *pour* temps *qui vienne*. (Desp., 144)

il n'y a . . . opiniastreté *si* grande et tardive *qu'*elle *soit*, à laquelle . . . (Vair, 160); Il n'y a personne, *pour si peu* judicieux et clair-voyant *qu'*il *soit*, qui ne juge à l'œil que . . . (Vair, 136) (Concessive and conditional. Compare *pour peu que* conditional: Que ne peuvent elles? Que craignent elles? *pour peu qu'*il y *ait* d'agencement à esperer en leur beauté, Mont., I, 71); *tant* peu *que* ce *soit* (Calv., O. F., 31); Ie n'en ay sceu trouver un *tant soit* il beau, riche ou grand seigneur, avec lequel mon cueur . . . se peust accorder (Marg., II, 35); nul ne se pourra plaindre . . . d'avoir été . . . offensé en sorte *que* ce *soit* (Calv., O. F., 27).

bon gré malgré *qu'*il en *eust**, je le mis à l'examen (Paliss., 96) (alternative); trouverent les cinq pelerins, lesquelz . . . emmenerent . . ., non obstant les exclamations, adjurations et requestes *qu'*ilz *feissent*. (Rab., G., 43-20); Or que ce que nous appellons mal ne le soit pas de soy, ou au moins *tel qu'*il *soit*, qu'il depende de nous de . . ., voyons s'il se peut maintenir. (Mont., I, 59) à *qui* ce *soit*, est bien de craindre . . . (Comm., I, 108); c'est tout un *qui* ce *fust** (Fail, P. R., 128); *qui qu'*ils *soient,* nous leur serons bien tenus. (Vair, 71); *quiconques* en *soit* l'aucteur, il est assez joly. (Desp., 105); *Quiconque* il *soit,* il en sort avecques perte. (Mont., III, 389)

Quoy que ce *soit* elle est grandement affligée. (Calv., R. C., ix); *Quoy qu'*il en *soit* et *qu'*il en *puisse* advenir, . . . je m'en suis aquitté (Est., 11); *Quoy que* je *reçoive* desagreablement me nuit (Mont., III, 409); *quoi que* je *sois,* je serai toujours votre . . . serviteur. (Malh., III, 44)

que chascun . . . se tiengne prest, sans soy esbahir de fortune *qui adviengne* (Comm., I, 83).

Quel que soyt le geolier, la prison . . . (Marg., III, 33); une famille esgarée, faisant . . . horreur *où qu'*elle *cerchast* à se placer (Mont., III, 355); là ny ailleurs *que* vous *alliez,* ie ne suis pas deliberée de iamais vous abandonner. (Marg., I, 171)

Relative Clauses

126. Expression of concession involving a relative clause may be compared with any other construction involving a relative clause. The mood of the relative clause is determined by the nature of the antecedent (although the reverse is true in some constructions, considered from the viewpoint of the reader only), and an indefinite antecedent is referred to in the subjunctive mood, as in many of the examples in §125. Here, however, our purpose is limited to a comparison of causative and concessive constructions involving *pour,* e.g.:

Ces nouvelles oyes, li sires de Biaumont ne vot plus demourer *pour* pryère c'on lui *peuist* faire, *pour* le grant désir qu'il *avoit* de venir à ce tournoy (Froiss., II, 99).

The relative clause modifying an indefinite antecedent, and introduced by *pour* causative, has the subjunctive:

Il y avoit aussy . . . deux gentilz hommes qui estoient allez aux baings, plus pour accompaigner les dames dont ilz estoient serviteurs que *pour* faulte qu'ilz *eussent* de santé. (Marg., I, 3); Malh., III, 397; Froiss., II, 52; Gaut., 615.

Likewise the concessive clause:

pour choses que *sceussent* oyr on ne les sçauroyt faire rire (Marg., II, 191); Desp., 207, 144; Chr., 1508.

The relative clause modifying a definite antecedent, and introduced by *pour* causative, has the indicative:

La ieune fille . . ., *pour* la paour qu'elle *avoit eue*, s'estoyt cachée soubz le lict (Marg., I, 36); Pissuthnes, . . . *pour* quelque amitié qu'il *portoit* à ceulx de Samos, luy envoya dix mille escus, à fin qu'il leur pardonnast (Amy., 41); Malh., III, 370; Gaut., 2696.

Owing to analogy the indicative also occurs in the concessive clause, after a definite antecedent:

Mais la Royne *pour* quelque intimité (?) qu'elle *portoit* à son pere ne luy faisoit pas fort bonne chere [i.e., à la fille]. (Marg., II, 29); Comm., I, 47.

Compare:

Ie ne croy pas, Hircan, dist Oisille, quelque chose que vous en dictes, que vous puissiez recepvoir nulle excuse d'elle. (*id.*, II, 20); A cui qu'ele onques vueut de mil; Ja nel savra ne cil ne cil. (Gaut., 3446)

The original distinction between causative and concessive construction appears to be based on this same distinction between antecedents which, in the *Heptaméron*, influences mood usage in both constructions. For instance, let us compare these two quotations from Gautier d'Arras:

> Valez, par Deu, ele n'iert pire
> Pour quanque vous l'avez gabee
> (Gaut., 2695)

> Ja preudom n'en iert pour lui pire,
> Pour quanqu'il onques set mesdire
> (*id.*, 1846)

In the first example the antecedent has a definite nature, whereas in the second it has an indefinite nature. In variant T the first example is distinguished as a causative construction, and the second as a concessive one:

> Pour ce que vous l'avez gabee
>
> Pour cose q̃ il en sache dire

It is doubtless apparent that, despite the similarities which we had noted between certain types of causative and concessive construction, no confusion of sense results. In concluding we may note that with reference to these constructions, there is a distinction between the use of *pour* and *par*. Although *pour* occurs in both, *par* occurs only in the causative:

ce que je ne dis *par* defiance que je *aye* de ta vertu (Rab., P., 8-42); plutôt *par* souffrance [tolérance] et coutume que *pour* aucun droit ni titre qu'ils en *eussent* (Malh., III, 417).

In this connection it is noteworthy that Malherbe prefers *pource que* to *parce que*, because of its obvious relationship to interrogative *pourquoi*. His usage shows *pour* after the indefinite or negative antecedent, as in the example above, or in

je ne vois point de sujet pourquoi vous ne puissiez, comme les autres, jouir de la gloire de votre labeur. (Malh., III, 241)

Résumé

127. In view of the general and ancient tendency of the language to employ the indicative in expressing facts and in view of the well-established practice of employing the subjunctive after the majority of the conditional conjunctions, one might expect the establishment of the indicative in the clause of real concession and of the subjunctive in the clause of supposed concession. This is not the case, however. On the contrary, the clause of real concession tends more and more to be stripped of its factual aspect and to be presented in the guise of a contingency expressed in the subjunctive, whereas the clause of supposed concession continues to be expressed not only in the subjunctive but in the conditional mood as well.

128. As a consequence of the decline of indicative usage after the concessive conjunctions, mood usage in the expression of concession tends to become more uniform during our period. After a given conjunction, however, it tends to persist. Following *quand*, for example, it remains essentially the same, although *quand*, after having served as either a conditional or a concessive conjunction, begins to drop its conditional sense and, at the other extremity, is compounded with *bien* and *encore*.

This decline of indicative usage, which is more rapid after 1550 than before, is rather a consequence of the supplanting of *combien que* by *bien que* and *encore que*, although, in addition, mood usage after *combien que* changes in favor of the subjunctive. After *encore que* the indicative is exceptional throughout the period. After *bien que* the indicative is rare; and we note a case of the indicative, in an edition of 1572 (Rons., A., 11), which is changed to the subjunctive in later editions (1578, 1587).

129. Examples of an apparently indifferent employment of mood occur throughout the century. Despite this indifference one might well hesitate to believe that the indicative and the subjunctive are employed with identical force. Attention has been called especially to an example of Palissy's practice, in §122. Froissart provides a more striking example:

Si en parla au roy . . . en faisant sa petition . . . à laquelle . . . condescendy le roy et son conseil et meismement le duc de Bourgoingne, pour tant que il luy sambloit que sa fille . . . en pourroit en temps advenir mieulx valloir, *non obstant que* plusieurs seigneurs de France en *parloient* ou *parlassent* en diverses manières et assés estrangement en disant: « A quel pourpos viennent ces Haynnuyers requérir, ne pryer le roy d'ayde? . . . » (Froiss., XV, 279)

Malherbe offers an explanation (§123) which would be more impressive if it were in accord with his own practice and which is more readily applicable in this case than in the one to which it was actually applied, since it is obvious that this example may not be interpreted as a purposeful illustration of indifference. Quite on the contrary, it appears to distinguish a real from a supposed concession, indicating, by a dual expression, that the author covers either situation; so that, substantially, the subjunctive serves as a counterbalance to the force of the indicative.

130. During the course of the sixteenth century concession becomes more firmly based on the employment of the subjunctive, which begins to be its common sign. Certain factors, however, such as the reality of an action or the nature of an antecedent, are still such persistent determinators that they prevent the crystallization of any broad and common rule envisaging a single, constant cause followed by an invariable result.

CHAPTER X

MISCELLANEA

Clauses Expressing Indirect Interrogation

131. After affirmative verbs, whether the clause is objective, subjective, or attributive in construction, we find the indicative, future, or conditional following *comme, comment, que* or *ce que, qui, dont*, and *pourquoi*. During our period *comment* tends to be replaced by *comme*, while both, as a second step, tend to be displaced by the conjunction *que*, conforming to the general tendency of the language to become more uniform in construction; but the employment of *comme* with the sense of *de quelle manière, combien*, or *à quel point* persists throughout the period in both direct and indirect interrogation. *Que* employed as an absolute relative pronoun, thus allowing it, like *qui*, to enter into indirect interrogation, also persists.

The subjunctive is exceptional both during and before our period. It is employed with potential force:

Et envoya le roy . . . devers luy Pierre Claret . . ., luy enchargeant fort en prendre quictance, affin que, pour le temps avenir, il fust veü et congneü *comme* le grand chambellan, chancellier, admiral et grand escuyer d'Angleterre, avec plusieurs autres, *eussent esté* pensionnaires du roy de France. (Comm., II, 243); Gaut., 3031 (*puisse*); Chr., 2148 (*facent*).

132. After negative verbs the subjunctive is more broadly persistent, but it becomes exceptional during our period, occurring less often than the indicative, future, or conditional:

je *ne* sçay *quoy* premier en luy je *doibve* admirer (Rab., G., 9-18); je *ne* voy poinct *comment* ce ne *soit* à nostre ruyne totale. (*id.*, G., 47-78); je *ne* vois point *comment* on *puisse* autrement entendre ce que dit saint Paul (Calv., O. F., 39); je *ne* voy point *pourquoy* . . . le poete ne se *puisse* servir de ce vocable (Est., 181); demora moult esgarée . . . comme celle qui *ne* savoit *que* elle *peuist* faire, ne que devenir. (Froiss., II, 38); Chr., 681, 3088, 4748; Gaut., 3610.

In these clauses the subjunctive ordinarily serves as a potential. In this usage the imperfect subjunctive is replaced by the conditional, and the present subjunctive by the conditional or the future:

ne sçavoit *comment* il *pourroit* contenter celui qui . . . (Comm., I, 207); La ville se depeuplant de bonnes maisons [riches], je *ne* sçay pas *que pourra* faire le pauvre peuple (Vair, 55); *ne* savoit *qu'*il y *trouveroit* (Froiss., II, 64).

The indicative is also employed:

je *ne* sçay *que* diable cecy *veult* dire (Rab., P., 14-30); ce mot de famulé, . . . elle *ne* sçavoit encores *qu'*il *vouloit* dire. (Desp., 51); Gaut., 2014 (*vaut**).

In expressing facts the indicative is employed even in the earlier language:

Mes *ne* set, *comant* il *a* non, Ne *qui* il *est* ne de quel jant (Chr., 2900); *id.,* 5183.

133. Expressions employed with concessive force must be considered apart. Their sense is ordinarily completed by the employment of the subjunctive mood:

du fait du roy d'Angleterre *ne leur challoit* au demourant *comme* il en *allast* (Comm., II, 43); *il ne luy chaloit qu'*elles *coustassent* (Desp., 81); Perrot . . . *ne se soucioit qui payast* (Fail, P. R., 149); Dom Mathurin . . ., qui *ne se soucioit pas qui coucheroit* avec . . . (*id.,* Eutr., 258); *il ne peut chaloir* de *quel* lieu il *soit* (Amy., 101).

Compare the inverted equivalent:

mais quelle qu'en soit la signification, il ne m'en chaut (Malh., III, 580).

When the sense is affirmative, the subjunctive is rare:

Il n'*importe* pas seulement qu'on voye la chose, mais *comment* on la *voye.* (Mont., I, 82)

Si *Implying Interrogation*

134. After this employment of *si* the subjunctive, which is exceptional in earlier works (e.g., Chr., 6212), disappears in our period, except as employed with conditional force:

ne sçay *si* vous *serez* point des miens (Desp., 24); je *ne* sais *s'*il le vous *aura mandé.* (Malh., III, 31); je *ne* sçay pas *s'*il m'*eust esté* possible (Est., 24).

But after expressions of concessive force we find the subjunctive:

Car *il ne peut chaloir si* celuy qui . . ., *soit* Roy ou homme de bas estat. (Calv., R. C., 764)

Optative Expressions

135. *Car* and *mar* of the older language (e.g., Gaut., 2213, 5020) have disappeared. *Mon vuel, suen vueil,* etc. (with subjunctive [Gaut., 647, 6505], future [Gaut., 5595; Chr., 6078], conditional [Gaut., 3575; Chr., 923]) persist in a new form:

Et *à la mienne volunté* que chascun *laissast* sa propre besoigne (Rab., P., Prol. -10 [cf. *utinam*, vous nous *baillez** nos cloches. *id.*, G., 19-27]); *A la mienne volonté*, qu'un chacun . . . *soit* . . . (Paliss., 24).

Vaugelas notes that in his time the court no longer employs this old manner of speaking, but, in its stead, *Plust à Dieu* (Vaug.-Chass., II, 452). In our period *pleust à Dieu* is, in fact, already the most common optative expression, followed next in order by *Dieu veuille.*

Optative Que

136. Professor Ritchie (*v.* §55) notes a rare and epic employment of optative *que* at the beginnings of the *chansons de geste* of the twelfth century (e.g., Oiez, seignor, *que* Deus vos seit aidanz!). It is also rare in other usages (e.g., Chr., 3997: *que* Des me confonde, Se . . .). In Froissart and in Commynes it is less rare (e.g., Froiss., II, 2; Comm., I, 219), but among the examples observed in our texts the first clear one which the context does not render in some manner subject to caution occurs in the *Heptaméron:*

Que à tous les diables soyt la villaine qui nous a faict d'une chose tant travailler (Marg., III, 35).

In this work optative *que* is employed approximately one tenth as many times as it is omitted. In Rabelais the proportion rises to one fifth. In Des Périers the change is abrupt: it is employed nearly as often as it is omitted. This work is also the first one in which the subject is not most frequently *Dieu, le diable, saint Antoine,* etc.:

Qu'*on* ne me vienne non plus faire des difficultez (Desp., 7); *id.*, 28, 73, 106, 110, 126, 171, 180, 187, 193.

In Ronsard's poetry optative *que* is extremely rare—twice as rare, comparatively speaking, as in the *Heptaméron*. In our later authors of the century it occurs approximately as often as in France's *L'Ile des Pingouins*.

137. The employment or omission of optative *que* is not subject to any apparent regulation:

Pleust à Dieu que eussiez dict la vérité! (Marg., I, 131); *Que* pleust à Dieu que tous les prestres de mon diocese n'en eussent non plus que luy! (Desp., 56); Je puisse mourir de male mort . . . si vous voulez maintenir ceste opinion (*id.*, 309); *Que* puisses tu estre plus heureux qu'Auguste (Amy., xxiv); *que* je voye comme ilz vous ont appris. (Desp., 73); La mort vienne sur eux, et *qu'*ils descendent vifs en enfer. (Calv., O. F., 95); *que* sainct Antoine me arde sy ceulx tastent . . .! (Rab., G., 27-61); le diable me faille si j'eusse failly de . . .! (*id.*, G., 39-69)

Yet the expressions in which it is omitted tend to become more and more stereotyped. At the end of our period, for example, in Malherbe's letters the subject is almost invariably *Dieu* (e.g., Dieu fasse que . . . . !). This usage in the second half of our period is not ordinarily the free usage of Gautier d'Arras:

> Or ni *ait* plus longe atendue,
> Mais lieve sus isnelement,
> Si qu'il n'i ait demourement.
> (Gaut., 156)

The difference is that it generally lacks imperative force.

138. Somewhat comparable to the construction involving optative *que* is the construction involving an interrogative and accusative *que* followed by the indicative, expressing regret or desire:

> Hé *que* ne suis je Ovide bien disant!
> (Rons., A., 21)
> *Que* ne puis-je estre Ovide bien disant!
> (*id.*, editions 1578, 1587)

Closely allied to the employment of the subjunctive without *que* is its employment to express a concession or a condition:

> Or *vienne* doncques ce qu'il en adviendra,
> I'en ay iecté le dé, là se tiendra
> Ma volunté sans aucun changement.
> (Marg., I, 179)

Dubitative Subjunctive

139. The dubitative usage of the subjunctive, which bears a close analogy to its usage in a relative clause having a negative antecedent, is not uncommon in our period:

Ie ne *sçaiche* chose qui[1] me doibve empescher (Marg., I, 113); vous . . . n'avez iamais aymé que l'on *ayt sceu* (*id.*, III, 194); il n'est encores imprimé, que je *saiche*. (Rab., P., 15-161); elle n'y fut jamais que je *sache* (Desp., 57); France, 152 (Jamais, qu'il me *souvienne*.)

---

[1] Compare *Il n'y a chose que je sache qui* (or: *ces Courtenay que vous savez qui prétendent* . . . [Malh., III, 101]), a construction so persistent that modern grammars still warn against it.

CHAPTER XI

GENERAL SUMMARY OF SUBJUNCTIVE USAGE

140. "Il est forcé de faire tort en detail qui veut faire droict en gros," says Montaigne. His words supply a commentary on the present chapter. It is inevitable that general statements concerning material of this character, even when they are based on a careful classification and examination of the details, should disregard and perhaps obscure a minority of very significant ones. Whatever values may exist in this study should not be sought so much in the few generalizations which follow as in the purposely minute examination of details and tendencies that has been carried out in the preceding chapters without confinement to the subject of subjunctive usage or even to that of mood usage in general.

After Declarative Expressions

141. *In objective clauses.* Comparatively speaking, it is after the suppositives that the subjunctive most commonly occurs. After affirmative employment mood usage remains erratic to some degree, but the subjunctive declines. After negative or conditioned employment, and after employment in negating circumstances, the subjunctive is usual.

The assertives, when affirmative, are followed by the subjunctive whenever there is an assimilation to the sense of the suppositives, whenever some determinative external influence exists, and in cases of attraction. They are also followed by the subjunctive when they occur in negating circumstances, and after ordinary negation, but in the latter case mood usage is erratic. After conditioned assertives subjunctive usage declines early in our period, whereas at the beginning mood usage is erratic.

The perceptives likewise, when negative, are occasionally assimilated to the sense of the suppositives. In such cases they are followed predominantly by the subjunctive. When they are conditioned, mood usage after them is erratic.

After negative verbs denoting expectancy the subjunctive remains the customary usage, but after affirmative employment subjunctive usage declines.

After negative verbs denoting certainty subjunctive usage tends to disappear early in our period. After conditioned employment mood usage remains erratic, but with the subjunctive becoming less predominant.

Mood usage is erratic after both ordinary and oratorical interrogation. It is likewise erratic after inherently negative verbs employed negatively, but after affirmative or interrogative employment of these verbs the subjunctive is predominant.

142. *In subjective clauses.* Mood usage is more stabilized in the subjective clause than in the objective clause. It is truly erratic only after non-affirmative expressions employed in the affirmative form. After affirmative expressions employed in the affirmative form the subjunctive occurs in inversions. The subjunctive is general after inherently negative expressions employed in either the affirmative or the negative form, after expressions occurring in negating circumstances, and after negation, interrogation, or condition.

After Expressions of Emotion

143. *In objective clauses.* After negative and interrogative construction the subjunctive is not invariable, but it is the predominant usage. After affirmative construction the subjunctive occurs, at the beginning of our period, in connection with expressions containing an element either of uncertainty or of volition, when the action of the subordinate clause is anticipated. From such cases subjunctive usage spreads into adverbial clauses expressing the cause, resulting in their assimilation to the objective clause and in a more extensive employment of the subjunctive.

144. *In subjective clauses.* Standardization of constructional practice begins to take place early in our period, and at the same time subjunctive usage becomes general.

After Expressions of Volition, Necessity, etc.

145. *In objective clauses.* After both direct and indirect expressions of volition the subjunctive is the usual usage. Exceptions occur after affirmative construction, but not after negation, interrogation, or condition. After expressions recognizable as belonging to the language of a governing body or final authority, indicating a resolution, a decision, or an arrangement, subjunctive usage declines during the latter part of our period, after affirmative but not after negative or conditioned construction.

146. *In subjective clauses.* The subjunctive is invariable in cases other than those somewhat special ones in which the condition depicted is not unfulfilled.

In Adverbial Clauses of Purpose

147. The subjunctive is invariable in the purpose clause. To express the facts more precisely, however, we may say that the purpose clause is invariably distinguished by subjunctive usage and that in our period it is rendered still more readily distinguishable by the increasing employment of conjunctive locutions serving as exclusive labels.

In Consecutive Clauses

148. In consecutive clauses of purpose, after conjunctive locutions expressing either manner or intensity, the subjunctive is employed after affirmative construction. It is also the ordinary usage after negation, interrogation, or condition, both in consecutive clauses of purpose and in those of result, and likewise after causative and related expressions.

In Comparative Clauses

149. At the beginning of our period mood usage in comparative clauses is erratic. During our period the subjunctive becomes exceptional.

In Temporal Adverbial Clauses

150. In connection with simultaneity the subjunctive is exceptional, but it persists after *comme, mais que,* and the negative

locution *sans que.* In connection with anteriority mood usage is erratic, except when we consider specific locutions such as *avant que,* after which mood usage ceases to be erratic.

In Causative Adverbial Clauses

151. After the affirmative conjunction *comme* subjunctive usage declines in the latter part of our period. After negative, interrogative, and conditioned conjunctions subjunctive usage persists.

In Adverbial Clauses of Concession

152. The employment of the subjunctive in concessive clauses increases during our period, reaching a point where it may be said that the subjunctive has become the common sign of the concessive construction.

Miscellanea

153. After verbs employed with concessive force the subjunctive is the ordinary usage in clauses expressing indirect interrogation and after interrogative *si.* After other expressions it persists with potential force only, except in clauses expressing indirect interrogation after negative verbs, where it persists, exceptionally also, as a true subjunctive.

Summary

154. From these facts, which constitute one phase of the syntactical history of the language preceding the classical period, it is evident that the syntax of the personal moods is quite extensively fixed or stabilized in the period from Commynes to Malherbe. In that portion which is not stabilized, the number of instances in which a distinct major tendency is discernible is large in comparison with the number in which usage is erratic. Fewest in number are the instances of absolute change in mood usage, and one would hardly expect to find many in the course of a period encompassing a single century, although this period of the history of the French language, standing as it does between

the Middle Ages and the height of the classical period in the seventeenth century, is by definition a period of change.

Modal syntax, being a subject too inconspicuous to attract the attention of contemporary students or reformers in more than an incidental manner, is by virtue of its inconspicuousness one of the subjects whose study reveals perhaps most accurately the gradual processes leading to the crystallization of the language, the multiplicity of these processes, and their interrelated unity. This study is concluded with the hope that the basic principles of this syntax and the details of its development during this period have been accurately discerned and effectively illustrated.

The opinions quoted in the Preface have, in the sixteenth century itself, counterparts which invite quotation at this point:

S'il est vray que toutes choses ont eu commencement, il est certain que la langue grecque, semblablement la latine, ont été quelque temps incultes et sans reigle de grammaire, comme est de present la nostre. (Geoffroy Tory, *Champ fleury* [Paris, 1529], fol. IV, v°.)

Mais je diray bien que nostre langue n'est tant irreguliere qu'on voudroit bien dire: veu qu'elle se decline, si non par les noms, pronoms et participes, pour le moins par les verbes, en tous leurs tens, modes et personnes. Et si elle n'est si curieusement reiglée, ou plus tost liée et gehinnée en ses autres parties, aussi n'ha elle point tant d'hetheroclites et anomaux, monstres etranges de la grecque et de la latine. (Joachim du Bellay, *Défense et illustration de la langue française* [ed. Henri Chamard, Paris, 1904], p. 111)

The results of a comparative study of some thirty thousand examples of usage show that in its modal syntax the language was already more regular than even Du Bellay perhaps believed, and that, as Darmesteter and Hatzfeld suggest, it possessed distinctive characteristics not unworthy of study and definition.

APPENDIX

SUPPLEMENTARY OBSERVATIONS BASED ON CALVIN'S *INSTITUTION*

The examination of the remainder of Calvin's *Institution*, undertaken for the reason mentioned in the Introduction, reveals examples of modal syntax contrary to that of the corresponding examples employed in §§7, 11, and 34:

§7: ilz *imaginent* que la Foy *soit* formée, quand . . . (208).

§11: il *n'allegue* point que Dieu *a* rendu . . . (477); Et *ne* peut-on *alleguer*, qu'il n'y *a* eu autre Sacrement (599).

§34: il *pourra advenir*, que quelqu'un *face* . . . (795).

This examination reveals also, of course, a great many confirmative examples. Among these examples it appears pertinent to cite especially the ones related to §§2, 30, 33, 34, 48, 85, 118, 122, and 124:

§2: il ne suffit pas de *croyre*, que Dieu *est* veritable, qu'il ne *puisse* mentir ne tromper: . . . (190).

§30: Qu'il n'*ayt* voulu autre chose dire, *il appert* de la sentence qu'il avoit mise un peu au paravant. (363); *Que ainsi soit* non seulement nostre Seigneur leur a faict les mesmes benefices qu'il nous fait, mais aussi . . . (436).

§33: Car *il semble* que cela n'*est* rien dire sinon que . . . (479).

§34: *possible* est que . . . il ne *pourvoyoit* pas mal à son Eglise (651).

§48: *Ce* qu'il evite la mort, cela luy tourne à plus grande destresse, que s'il eust eu à mourir cent foys. (441)

§85: *Pour* faire fin, *et que* nous ne *ayons* à repeter . . . (702); les bonnes œuvres sont cause [affirmative antecedent] *pourquoy* nostre Seigneur *fait* bien à ses serviteurs (390).

§118: Et ce *n'est pas pource que* la Parolle ne *soit* assez ferme (565); Car les iniques *ne* craignent point Dieu, *pource qu'ilz ayent* crainte d'encourir son offence, . . .: mais *pource qu'ilz scaivent* qu'il est puissant à se venger

(199); 48; 148; 152; 565; *non pas pource qu'*il *ayt* souffert selon la divinité: mais *par ce que* le Christ . . . luy mesme . . . *estoit* Dieu . . . (639).

§122: Et *combien que* nous *verrons* tantost plus amplement, combien elle differe de la verité de la Foy: neantmoins il ne nuyra de rien, . . . (188).

§124: *quand bien* nous y *aurions satisfaict,* encores sommes nous serviteurs inutiles (410).

The numerous remaining confirmative examples fall into two groups: (1) duplicates of the expressions and constructions covered by the material preceding this Appendix, which are listed in the Index; and (2) new or additional expressions and constructions. The latter, listed below, supplement the list of expressions and constructions supplied in the Index.

ADDITIONAL EXPRESSIONS AND CONSTRUCTIONS

Arranged in alphabetical order according to the key words, which are italicized. Numerical references in parentheses indicate pages in the *Institution.* Abbreviations: C, conditional; F, future; I, indicative; S, subjunctive; SC, subjunctive (ordinarily pluperfect) with conditional force; X, indeterminate form.

A

il n'y a nulle *absurdité* en cela; que (413: S).

accordons-leur . . . que (676: S).

cela est vulgaire et *accoustumé,* que (682: I).

c'est une chose trop incertaine et mal seure, d'*affermer* que (611: S).

non pas que nous veuillons *affermer* que (612: S).

si quelqu'un *ayme mieux* que (723: S).

quand *ainsi* seroit, que (797: C).

si on *allegue* que (143: S).

il n'*allegue* point que (477: I).

ne peut-on *alleguer,* que (599: I).

cela *appartient* à sa gloire, que (785: S).

n'*appercevans* point que (581: I).

je n'*approuve* point, que (185: S).

je m'esmerveille de quelle hardiesse ilz osent *asseurer*, que (316: S).

qu'ilz n'*attendent* [s'attendent] point que (156: S).

jà soit qu'il soit bien advis [*avis*], que (797: S).

il ne nous semble point advis [*avis*], que (122: S).

B

ne fault qu'ilz *babillent*, que (740: I).

le Seigneur nous fera ce *bien*, que (182: F).

le *but* est, que (306: S).

C

encores que nous posions le *cas*, que (382: S).

non pas à *cause* que (309: S).

nous n'obtenons point salut, à *cause* que (210: S).

elle sera *cause* que (751: F).

ne fault point que quelqu'un *caville* icy, que (435: I).

il nous soit *certain*, que (575: I).

que nous ayons donc cela pour *certain*, que (176: I).

il ne fault pas petite asseurance, pour rendre quelqu'un *certain* que (648: S).

nous rendront-ilz donc *certains*, que ? (671: S).

que le vin soit rouge ou blan, c'est tout un, et ne peut *challoir* (668).

il n'en peut gueres *chaloir* . . . que (357: S).

il ne peut *chaloir* quelz . . . (751: I).

il ne peut *challoir* qui (162: I).

Sainct Cypryan *combat* fort, que (695: I).

nul ne *combat* maintenant, que (683: S).

le *commandement* . . . est, que (709: S).

cela vault autant *comme* qui diroit (330).

à fin qu'ilz ne se *compleignent* que (702: S).

nous *concederons* . . . que (386: I).

s'ilz veullent *conclure* que (614: I).

qui est-ce qui ne pourra *conclurre* . . . que (170: I).

ceste *condition*, que (404, 556: S).

par ceste seule *condition* que (592: S).

soubz *condition* que (324: S).

ilz ayment donc mieux . . ., que *confesser* que (699: S).

s'il *confessent* que (104: S).

il nous enseigne de ne nous point *confier*, que (539: S).

il y a icy deux choses à *considerer.* . . . que (336: S).

si nous *considerons* que (815: I).

ce qui *consiste* en deux choses. . . . que (693: S).

de là nous reviendra une . . . *consolation*, que (822: F; 800).

ilz ne *constituent* point quand (311: F).

la parolle de Sainct Paul nous doibt *contenter:* que (750: I).

ces deux choses sont *contraires:* que (473: S).

ne *contrevient* point que (201: X).

il n'est pas *convenable* que (93: S).

il n'est pas *convenant*, . . . que (718: S).

Jesus Christ . . . nous *convie* et nous monstre par son exemple que (646: S).

il ne fault *craindre*, que (491: S).

pour faire à *croyre* que (102: I).

il ne suffit pas de *croyre*, que (190: I, S).

D

il a *determiné* que (481: S)

ne sont elles pas bien *dignes*, que (809: S).

il nous reputera *dignes* que (806: S).

scauroit-on imaginer chose plus malheureuse; que *dire*, que (442: S).

cela surmonte toute misere, de *dire* que (442: S).

si nous *disons* que (794: S; 795: I).

ce n'est pas à *dire* que (610: S).

il y a bien à *dire*, que (735: S).

je laisse à *dire,* que (205: I).

c'est un erreur trop evident, de *dire* que (619: S).

c'est . . . une calumnie trop frivole, de *dire* que (402: X).

car de *dire* que (608: S), c'est une moquerie.

il *dispense* et ordonne . . . que (481: S).

comme si quelqu'un *disputoit*, que (429: I).

pour laquelle cause il est dict [*dit*], que (515: S).

il n'est pas dict [*dit*] que (600: S).

il n'y a point de *doubte*, que (492: F; 818: X).

il ne *doubtera* pas que (509: X, F; 510: I).

E

elle ne pourra eschapper [*échapper*], que (115, 652: S).

il nous fault . . . *efforcer* à cela, que (811: S).

ce scrupule n'*empesche* de rien, à ce que (680: S).

l'entendement . . . n'est pas *empesché*, que (195: S).

il n'y aura nul *empeschement*, que (454: S; 198: X).

il [un commandement] *emporte* que (305: S).

enseigner [volitional] que (371, 561, 748: S; 197, 561: X).

je n'ay peu conprendre comment ilz *entendent* que (680: S).

comment *entendent*-ilz que (321: S).

si nous *entendons* que (357: S).

Daniel . . . n'a pas voulu *entendre* que (345: S).

qui est-ce qui *esperera;* que (798: S).

de nous faire *estimer* que (196: I).

plusieurs trouvent *estrange*, pourquoy (746: X).

quelle *excuse* donc avons-nous que (599: X).

et ne peuvent *excuser* que (685: S).

je demande s'ilz se peuvent *excuser*, que (102: S).

le plus *expedient* seroit, que (695: S).

qui nyera cela estre *expedient*, que (803: S).

F

il se peut *faire*, qu'il aura pris . . . (386).

comment donc se pourroit-il *faire* que (721: S).

s'il se povoit *faire*, que (545: S).

faire: elles feront que (571: F).

jamais . . . nous ne parvenons à ceste *felicité*, que (194: S).

la *fin* est que (159, 376, 539: S; 154: I).

la *fin* est à ce que (486: X).

G

se donnent de *garde*, que (422, 575: S).

un Payen se *glorifioit* que (569: I).

I

combien qu'ilz n'*ignorassent* point que (766: I).

ilz *ignorent* que (55: S).

ilz *imaginent* que (208: S).

nous ne devons pas *imaginer* que (517: S).

je desire d'*impetrer* . . . que (470: X).

qu'il ne nous puissent *imposer*, que (403: S).

si nous ne luy voulons *imputer* que (346: S).

il signifie estre *indifferent* de quelle . . . (754: S).

il est *indubitable* que (202: I).

infere-il que (537: S).

si quelqu'un . . . vouloient *inferer* . . . que (495: I).

c'est une moquerie, d'*inferer* que (474: S).

il avoit esté *institué* . . . que (651: S).

si quelqu'un ha ceste vraye *intelligence* que (714: S).

ilz n'osent pas simplement *interpreter*, que (320: S).

J

jacoit que (96: S).

jusques après que (94: S).

L

il n'est *licite* que (785: S).

ce n'est pas chose *licite*, que (788: S).

cela ne laisse point d'avoir *lieu* entre nous, que (147: S).

il fault prendre . . . avec certaine *limitation*, c'est, que (320: S).

qu'il y ayt une seconde Loy [*loi*]. C'est, que (523: S).

l'Eunuche demande . . . s'il n'est pas *loisible* que (615: S).

M

quel *mal* y a il; que (351: S).

se *malcontentoient* que (701: I).

malgré qu'ilz en ayent (103).

maulgré qu'il en eust (808).

lequel seroit le *meilleur*, que (695: X).

voire mesmes [*même*] que (798: S).

si nous *meritons*, que (205: S).

ce n'est pas si grand' *merveille*, de quoy (397: I).

ce n'est point de *merveilles* que (295: I).

quel *mestier* estoit-il; que (785: S).

s'il est *mestier* que (812: S).

il *met* [par écrit] que (704: I).

c'est une *mocquerie* . . . que (174: S).

les *moindres* concupiscences qui (172: S).

cela est une chose semblable à un *monstre*, que (815: I).

Jesus Christ . . . nous *monstre* . . . que (646: S).

aucuns s'efforcent de *monstrer*, que (533: S).

cela ne fait rien pour *monstrer* que (389: X, S).

on ne scauroit *monstrer* . . . , que (601: S).

ilz ont inventé un *moyen* . . . C'est, que (648: S).

il fault tousjours tenir ce *moyen*, que (319: S).

N

qu'ilz me respondent donc; s'ilz peuvent nyer [*nier*], que (102: S).

pourrons nous nyer [*nier*] que (56: S).

s'il est donc *notoire*, que (407: I).

c'est chose *notoyre*, que (187: C).

ce n'est pas chose *nouvelle:* que (621: S).

O

ne fault pas que quelqu'un *objecte* que (637: I).

il fault rejetter de noz espritz ceste faulse *opinion*, que (714: S).

s'il n'est *ordonné* que (506: S).

cela est . . . *osté* aux calumniateurs, que (403: S).

n'*ostons* point cela à la Loy de Dieu, que (410: S).

oublier que (116: I).

P

il n'est jamais *parlé* . . . que (601: S).

quelle impudence seroit-ce; de *penser* que (798: I).

si nous *pensons* que (815: I).

voulant *persuader* que (656: I).

est ce *peu* de chose . . . que (172: S).

ilz se *plaignent* que (148: I).

il repute, que . . . est en ce *point* estably, que (536: S).

la reigle . . . *porte* cela, que (169: S).

possible est que (651: I).

possible est que ce que (580: I).

ce n'est pas *pource que* (565: S).

pouvoir: see scay.

ilz *prennent pour certain*, que (403: I).

à fin que . . .: quand ilz *pretendront* que (134: S).

prevoyant [volitional] que (125: S).

ceux qui . . . ne *prient* que (552: S).

si c'est chose notoire, que cela *procede* . . ., que (413: S).

ce n'est point un petit *proffit*, que (802: S).

il n'y a pas maintenant grand *propos*, que (414: S).

il n'est pas encores *prouvé*, que (417: S).

voyons par quelz argumens ilz *prouvent,* que (313: S).

les Celestins . . . s'aydoient de . . ., pour *prouver* que (420: I).

ilz ont à *prouver* que (533: I).

par cela on ne peut *prouver* que (450: S).

Q

quand mesmes ilz auroient quelque Moyse pour Advocat (534).

c'est *que* [afin que] (814: S).

aucontraire *que* [si] (571: S).

mais *que* [pourquoi] ne nous assemblons-nous . . .? (147)

*qu'*est cela autre chose, sinon . . .? (332)

qu'est-ce que nous prenons aucune confiance ou gloire de noz œuvres? (388)

car *quelque* bien *que* [antecedent affirmative] promet le Seigneur (201).

quelque part *qu'*il y a promesse, la Foy y ha sur quoy s'appuyer (625).

s'il est *question* que (648: S).

il n'est pas *question* que (190, 745: S).

R

estoit-ce rayson [*raison*], que (705: X).

si c'est chose *raisonnable,* que (803: S).

l'Escriture nous *rameine* tousjours là, que (796: S).

lesquelles choses se *rapportent* toutes là, que (512: S).

nostre Seigneur Jesus a mis ceste *reigle* . . ., que (526, 590: S).

que sera ce, si nous respondons [*répondons*], que (109: I).

ilz nous *reprochent* que (640: I).

le Prophete *reprochoit* aux Israëlites: que (533: S).

ilz *reputoient* . . . que (456: I).

ceste donc icy est nostre *requeste* que (558: S).

je ne *requiers* pas, que (787: S).

il *reste* en après, que (204: S).

il nous fault donc scavoir et *retenir* que (589: I).

je demanderay . . . qui nous a *revelé* que (535: S).

S

je *scay* Seigneur, que la voye de l'homme n'est pas en son pouvoir: ne qu'il puisse dresser ses pas. [et qu'il n'est pas en son pouvoir qu'il puisse . . .] (503).

il est bien *seant* que (743: S).

le *sens* de l'Apostre . . . est . . . que (315: S).

il nous *serviroit* de bien peu, que (626: S).

seulement que nous luy donnions ouverture en nostre cœur pour la recevoir, et nous l'obtiendrons. (635)

il *signifie* [volitional], que (127: S).

cela ne *signifie* point que (86: S).

nous devons avoir une grande *solicitude*, que (562: S).

l'Escriture met la *somme* de nostre salut en ce poinct: que (199: S).

la *somme* est que (154, 303: S).

ne *songeons* point que (531: S).

un autre passage enseigne les serviteurs de ne se *soucier* de quel estat ilz soient (754).

qui est-ce qui *souffriroit;* que (702: S).

s'il nous *souvient*, que (153, 795: I).

encores ne *suffist*-il point, que (202, 443: S).

T

tant peu que ce soit (652).

il y a des *tesmoignages* . . . que (503: S).

il nous est . . . *tesmoing*, que (491: F).

ne cessons donc point de *tendre* là: que (788: X).

que nous *tenions* cela pour asseuré, que (409: I).

il a *tenu* à leur perversité, que (102: I).

les Israëlites ne se *tiendroient* point . . . que (117: S).

l'Apostre attribue ce *tiltre* . . . à l'Evangile, [veut] qu'il soit nommé parolle de la Foy (201).

cela n'est nullement *tollerable*, que (815: S).

c'est *tout un* qui ou quel en soit le messager (591; 158: X).

ilz craingnent et *tremblent* que (526: S).

tous ceux . . . *trouveront* pour certain que (367: I).

V

ilz ne se veulent pas *vanter* . . . que (419: S).

si c'est chose *veritable* que (570: I).

ceste est la perpetuelle *verité* [logical necessity] d'un corps, que (638: S).

cecy est aussi une grande *vertu:* que (790: S).

l'Escriture *veut bien* que (809: S).

je ne *voiz* point donc, pourquoy (143: S).

il n'y a que ceste *voye*, par laquelle on puisse parvenir . . .: à scavoir, que (795: S).

s'il est donc *vray*, que (102: I; 204: S).

il n'est pas non plus *vray semblable* que (593, 808: S).

combien est-il plus *vraysemblable;* que . . .? (739: S)

vulgaire: see accoustumé.

INDEX OF EXPRESSIONS AND CONSTRUCTIONS

The expressions and constructions listed below are drawn from the pages indicated in the Bibliography of Authors. A supplementary list of those taken from Calvin's *Institution* appears in the Appendix. For the sake of completeness this index refers occasionally to the previously published material mentioned in the Introduction. The items are arranged in the alphabetical order of their key words, which are italicized.[1] Numerals refer to sections dealing either with the type of example shown or with a related type.

ABBREVIATIONS

I   followed by the indicative, excluding the future.
F   followed by the future.
C   followed by the conditional.
S   followed by the subjunctive.
SC   followed by the subjunctive (ordinarily pluperfect) employed with the force of the conditional.
X   followed by an indeterminate form.
c   added to one of the abbreviations above, indicates occurrence in a conditional sentence.
n.   negative verb.
nc.   employed in negating circumstances (e.g., §19).
?   interrogative.
(p.) preceded by.
(vol) volitional employment.
[ ]   brackets enclose items and usages drawn from material outside the period from Commynes to Malherbe, that is, from Chrétien de Troyes, Gautier d'Arras, Jean Froissart, or Anatole France. The name of the latter is also invariably inclosed, in order to distinguish modern material from material preceding the period.
adj. adjective.
adv. adverb.

PQ *Philological Quarterly*, X (1931), 294-306.
RR Supplement to the *Romanic Review*, 1931.

[1] The orthography of the example of latest date is usually employed, and that of the earliest examples is occasionally modernized to serve better the purpose of the Index.

A

il s'y coula un *bruit* que, I; 7, 31.

le *bruit* court que, il court un bruit que, I, F, [I, France]; 7, 31.

le *bruit* est que, il est un bruit que, il est grand bruit que, I, C; 7, 31.

il n'est point de *bruit* que, S; 13, 37.

semer un *bruit* que, I; 7.

leur *but* est que, S; 59.

C

[n. *cacher* que, I, C, France]; 17.

calumnier que, I, X; 7.

car; 117.

car (optative); 135.

au *cas* que (conditional), [I, F, S], S, X, [S, France]; *RR* 15.

au *cas* que (concessive), I, S; 122.

en *cas* que, I, C, S, X; *RR* 15.

c'est grand *cas* que, X; 32.

mettre le *cas* que, X; 2.

posé le *cas* que, le cas posé que, S, X; *RR* 15.

poser le *cas* que, S; 2.

prendre le *cas* que, S, X; 2.

à *cause* que, I, X; 117.

être *cause* que, I, C, X; 101.

n. devoir être *cause* que, S; 60, 101.

n. être sans *cause* que, I; 32.

pour *cause* que, I; 117.

[pour la *cause* de ce que, I]; 117.

causer que, I, C, X; 101.

ce (this fact); 48; *see* se plaindre que.

ce que (in indirect interrogation); 131.

[n. pouvoir se *celler* que, S]; 101.

cependant que, cependent que, ce pendant que, ce pendent que, I, F, C, X; 110.

être *certain* que (personal subject), [I, F], I, C, X, [X, France]; 7.

être *certain* que (impersonal subject), [I], I, Cc, SC, X, [I, X, France]; 31.

être chose *certaine* que, [X], I, Fc; 31.

trouver *certain* que, I; 7.

certifier que, [C], I, C, [C, France]; 7.

n. *chaloir* à qlqn comme, S; 133.

[n. *chaloir* à qlqn quand, S]; 133.

n. *chaloir* à qlqn que (ce que), S; 133.

n. *chaloir* à qlqn quel . . . (noun), X; 133.

n. pouvoir *chaloir* de quel . . . (noun), S; 133.

n. pouvoir *chaloir* si, S; 134.

chanter que, I; 7.

donner *charge* à qlqn que (vol), X; 59.

donner *charge* (accuser) qlqn que, I; 7.

à la *charge* que, F, C; *RR* 15.

être la *charge* de qlqn qu'il, X; 59.

[être *chargé* que (personal subject), S]; 56.

[*charger* que (vol), S]; 56.

charger (accuser) que, I; 7.

charger (accuser) qlqn de ce que, I; 7.

[avoir *cher* que, S]; 56.

[n. devoir faire *chiere* que, S]; 11.

chose que, ce que, que; 48.

être . . . (adj.) . . . *chose* que: *see* the adjective.

avoir le *cœur* amer que: *see* amer.

[*com* . . . que (concessive), S]; 125.

combien que; 121, 122, 128.

[être *commandé* que, S]; 56.

donner *commandement* que, S, X; 59.

faire *commandement* que, [S, X], S, X; 59.

commander que, [S, X], C, S, X; 56, 57, 69.

comme with concessive expressions; 133.

n. vouloir *confesser* que, S; 11.

avoir une *confession* que, I; 7.

avoir *confiance* que, I; 7.

[*confier* que, I, France]; 7.

[donner *congé* que, S]; 61.

c'est quelque *conjecture* que, F; 31.

conjecturer que, I, S, [X, France]; 2.

conjurer que, S, X; 56, 58.

n. avoir *connaissance* que, S; 13.

connaître (savoir), Gaut., Froiss., Comm., Rons.

connaître que, [I], I, F, C, S, X, [I, France]; 1.

connaître que (p. si), I, S, X; 24.

n. *connaître* que, X; 8.

donner à *connaître* que, I, X; 7.

faire *connaître* que, I, X, [I, France]; 7.

n. *connaître* quel . . . (noun) . . . ce, X; 132.

être *connu* comme (impersonal), SC; 131.

avoir *conscience* que, X; 7.

[avoir *conseil* que, avoir un conseil que, C]; 63, 64.

[donner *conseil* que, donner un *conseil* que, S]; 59.

[être *conseillé* que (impersonal), C, S]; 56, 63, 64.

[être *conseillé* à ce que (personal subject), C]; 55, 56.

[*conseiller* comme, S]; 131.

conseiller que, [S, X], I (devoit), C, S, X; 56, 57; *P&*6, 7.

[n. *conseiller* que, S]; 60.

bailler *consentement* que, X; 61.

consentir que, I; 7.

consentir que (vol), [S], S, X; 61.

n. *consentir* que, [S], S, X; 62.

vouloir *consentir* que (p. si), X; 62.

n. vouloir *consentir* que, X; 62.

vouloir à grand peine *consentir* que, S; 62.

il est *consequent* que, X; 32.

consideré que, I; 117.

[fut regardé et *consideré* que, S]; 59.

considerer que, [I], I, F, C, SC, X, [I, France]; 7.

n. *considerer* que, I, Fc, X; 14.

recevoir une *consolation* que; 46.

[*constater* que, I, France]; 7.

fut *constitué* que, X; 64.

contendre que, I, Cc; 7.

être *content* que, S, X; 46.

se *contenter* que, I, X; 46.

n. *contester* que, S; 17.

[paraître à qlqn *contraire* à toute discipline que, S, France]; 75.

[*contredire* que, S]; 16.

[nc. *contredire* que (vol), S]; 60.

n. *contredire* que (vol), X; 60.

n. savoir *contredire* que (vol), S; 60.

se *contrister* de ce que; 45, 46, 48.

être *convenable* que, S; 75.

n. être *convenable* que, X; 75.

convenir que, I; 7.

convenir que (impersonal), S; 75.

n. *convenir* que (impersonal), X; 75.

[*convenir* à qlqn que (impersonal), S, X]; 75.

[n. *convenir* à qlqn que (impersonal), S]; 75.

[n.? *convenir* à qlqn que, X]; 75.

[se *convenir* que (vol), S]; 61.

[*convoiter* que, couvoitier que, coveitier que, S]; 56.

[venir en *corage* à qlqn que, S]; 77.

corner que, S; 3 or 59 (1).

[n. être la *coulpe* de qlqn que, I]; 32.

donner *courage* à qlqn qu'il, X; 59.

[li *couraige* m'en siet trop bien que, F]; 7.

[se *courroucer* (correcier) de ce que]; 45, 46.

vouloir qu'il *coûte* beaucoup que, S; 56.

[être *coutume* (que), X]; 32.
[être *coutume* à qlqn que, I]; 32.
[être *coutume* de qlqn que, X]; 32.
ce n'est de *coutume* que, S; 75.
étant la *coutume* que, S; 59, 75.
[être (qlqn) *coustumiers* qu'il, S];
  32, 75.
[mettre en *covenant* que, F, C]; 7.
craindre que, [S], Cc, S, X, [S, X,
  France]; 46.
n. *craindre* que, S, Xc; 50.
[n.? *craindre* que, S, France]; 46, 50,
  51.
n. devoir *craindre* que, X; 50.
falloir *craindre* que, S; 46.
il est à *craindre* que, S, X; 46.
se *craindre* que, X; 46.
crainte que; 46.
de *crainte* que; 84, 86.
avoir *crainte* que, X; 46.
n. avoir *crainte* que, S; 50.
[n. être la *crainte* de qlqn que, X];
  46.
[exprimer la *crainte* que, S, France];
  46.
[avoir sa *créance* que, S]; 5.
sa *creance*, qui estoit que, X; 5, 7.
faire *cri* que: *see* ban.
crier que, I, C, [I, France]; 7.
crier que (vol), S, X; 59.
faire *crier* que (vol), [S], S, X; 59.
c'est chose difficile à *croire* comme,
  X; 131, 132.
croire que; 2, 43, 122.
croire que (p. si), I, S, X, [I,
  France]; 26.
? *croire* que, [I], I, S, X, [I, C, S,
  France]; 21.
n. *croire* que, I, S, X, [S, France];
  10.
nc. *croire* que, S; 19.
[n. *croire* que (p. si), S, France]; 10,
  26.

n.? *croire* que, F, X [C, France]; 22.
? *croire* et se persuader que, S; 22.
pouvoir *croire* que, C; 7.
? pouvoir *croire* que, S, [F, France];
  22.
n. pouvoir *croire* que, S, X; 10.
n. savoir *croire* que, S, X; 10.
vouloir *croire* que, F; 7.
n. vouloir *croire* que (p. si), S; 10.
faire *croire* que (supplementing
  croire que), I, S, X, [X, France]; 2.
devoir faire *croire* que, I; 7.
? penser faire *croire* que, S, X; 22.
n. penser faire *croire* que, S; 10.
vouloir faire *croire* que (p. si), S; 26.
? vouloir faire *croire* que, S; 22.
falloir *croire* que, I, C; 7.
il est à *croire* que, I, Ic, F, SCc, X;
  31.
il n'est pas à *croire* que, I; 14, 37.
il est aisé à *croire* que, I, C; 31.
avoir de la peine à *croire* que, S; 19.
faire accroire (ac*croire*) que [C], I,
  X; 2, 7.
se faire accroire (ac*croire*) que, I; 2,
  7.
? faire à *croire* que, S, X; 22.
n. faire accroire (ac*croire*) que, S;
  10.
n. savoir faire à *croire* que, X; 10.
n. savoir faire accroire (ac*croire*)
  que, X; 10.
vouloir faire accroire (ac*croire*) que,
  C; 2, 7.
se faire à *croire* que, I, F; 7.
nc. de *croire* que, S; 19.
est de *croire* que, I; 7.
il n'est pas difficile de *croire* que, S;
  19.
cela est indigne du sens commun de
  croire que, S; 19.
il est permis de *croire* que (p. si), S;
  26

se dispenser de *croire* que, F; 19.

[feindre de *croire* que, I, France]; 7, 19.

il est *croyable* que, I; 31.

[c'est chose *croyable* que, SC]; 31.

comment est-il *croyable* que? S; 38.

[*croyance* que, I, X, France]; 7.

[venir *cuers* à qlqn que, S]; 77.

[*cuider* (que), I]; 2.

cuider que; 2, 122.

cuider: se cuida mettre à estudier (Rab.); M. de Bressieu en a cuidé mourir (Malh.).

[*cuider* que (p. quand), S]; 26.

[*cuider* que (p. qui), S]; 26.

[*cuider* que (p. si), S, X]; 26.

? *cuider* que, [S, X], F, C, S, X; 22.

n. *cuider* que, [S, X], S, X; 10.

[n. *cuider* que (p. si), X]; 10, 26.

[devoir *cuider* que, S]; 2.

[cuidier (*cuider*) et antandre que, C]; 7.

[*cuider* et croire que, I, S]; 2.

[*cuider* et croire que (p. si), S]; 26.

[*cuider* et croire et penser que, S]; 2.

[cuidier (*cuider*) et s'an prisier que, S]; 2.

[mettre *cure* que, S]; 59.

[mettre sa *cure* en ce que, S]; 59.

D

[n. deignier (*daigner*) que, S]; 62.

y avoir *danger* que, S, X; 78.

? y avoir *danger* que, S; 78.

être *danger* que (impersonal), S; 78.

être en *danger* que, F (conjectural); cf. 32.

le *danger* était que, X; 32.

davant que, S, X; 112.

débattre que, I, X; 7.

estimer *decent* et sain que, X; 61.

déclarer que, I, F, C, X, [I, France]; 7.

déclarer que (p. sans), X; 20.

[*déconseiller* et défendre que, S]; 56.

découvrir que, I; 7.

mettre en avant un *décret* que, S, X; 64.

proposer un *décret* que, S, X; 64.

être *décrété* que, C; 64.

être *décrété* que (p. si), S; 67.

n. prendre à *dédain* que, S; 62.

[n. le tenir à *dédain* que, I]; 32, 62.

deduire que, I; 7.

défendre que, [S], S, X; 56.

faire *défendre* que, X; 56.

n. pouvoir se *défendre* que, X; 60.

[n. avoir *défense* que, S]; 60.

[mettre sus une ordonnance et *défense* que, S]; 64.

être en *défiance* que; 46.

n. se *défier* que, SC; 50.

deliberer que, C; 64.

délibérer si, C; 134.

demander que, I, S, X; 56, 57.

ne *demeura* guère que (quand), ne demeura gaires de jours, que, [I], X; *see* que.

[n. *demeurer* que, S]; 72.

[*demeurer* (tarder) à qlqn que, X]; 77.

démontrer que, I, [I, F, France]; 7.

denoncer que, I, F, C; 7.

denoncer que (vol), S; 59.

avoir despit (*dépit*) que, X; 46.

déplaire à qlqn que, I, X; 46.

prendre sans *déplaisir* que, S; 61.

[être *déplorable* que, S, France]; 46.

[deproiier (*déprier*) que, S, X]; 56.

depuis que; 109.

le *dernier* qui, X; *PQ* 16.

le *dernier* . . . (noun) . . . que, I; *PQ* 16.

le *dernier* . . . (noun) . . . qui, I; *PQ* 16.

[*des* que, C]; 117.

n. *désigner* que, X; 11.
avoir *desir* que, S, X; 59.
n. avoir *desir* que, X; 60.
n. aller *desirant* que, X; 60.
desirer que, [S], S, X, [S, France];
56, 71.
n. *desirer* que, S; 60.
[*desservir* que (p. qui), S]; 62.
[*desservir* (que), S]; 61.
être la *destinée* telle que, S; 75.
[n. pouvoir *destraindre* que, S]; 60.
[*detenir* que, S]; 56.
quelle *detestation* que, S; 32, 53.
detester que: *see* abomination.
devant que, [I, S], S, X; 112.
[*devant* ce que, S]; 112.
[*deviner* que, I, France]; 7.
[par tel *devise* que (result), F]; 92.
[par tel *devise* que (purpose), S, X];
88.
être *difficile* que (impersonal), S; 35.
la *difficulté* est que, I; 118.
être *digne* que, S; 61.
être *digne* que (p. si), X; 62.
être *digne* duquel, S, X; 61.
se juger *digne* que, S; 61.
[rendre *diligence* que, S]; 59.
dire que, [I, F, C, S, X], I, F, C, S,
SC, X, [I, France]; 3, 46.
dire que (p. si), I, X; 27.
? *dire* que, S, X; 22.
n. *dire* que, [I, S, X], I, F, S, SC, X,
[I, X, France]; 11.
n. ? *dire* que, I, SC, X, [I, France];
22.
dire que (vol), [I, S, X], S, X, [X,
France]; 3, 59, 69.
n. *dire* que (vol), X; 60.
n. ? *dire* que (vol), S, X; 60.
dire paroles (parolles . . . dictes)
que, S, X; 59.
[n. devoir *dire* que, S]; 11.
n. falloir *dire* que, I; 14.

laisser *dire*, I; 3.
? oser *dire* que, S; 22.
ouïr *dire* que, X; 3.
? ouïr *dire* que, S; 22.
n. ouïr *dire* que, S, X; 11.
à grand peine ouïr jamais guieres
dire que, X; 20.
pouvoir *dire* que, [I], I, X; 3.
n. pouvoir *dire* que, [S], S, X; 11.
il se peut *dire* que, I; 3.
? savoir *dire* que, S; 22.
[n. savoir *dire* que, S]; 11.
sembler *dire* que, I; 3.
vouloir *dire* que, I, C, S; 3.
vouloir *dire* que (p. si), S; 27.
? vouloir *dire* que, I, S, SC; 22.
n. vouloir *dire* que, S; 11.
vouloir *dire* (prétendre) que (p.
encore que), X; 27.
[vouloir *dire* tant que (p. si), S]; 27.
est-ce à *dire* que? S; 22.
de *dire* que, F; 3, cf. 20.
nc. de *dire* que, S; 20.
de *dire* que! S; 46, cf. être aise de
savoir que, 46.
se garder de *dire* que, S; 20.
c'est mensonge de *dire* que, S; 20.
c'est reverie de *dire* que, S; 20.
[*dire* et conjurer que (vol), X]; 59.
dire et maintenir que, I; 3.
[n. *dire* et raconter que, S]; 11.
discourir que, C; 7.
n. *dissimuler* que, I; 17.
n. *dissimuler* que (vol), X; 60.
? être mal *dit* que, I; 22.
n. être mal *dit* que, I; 14.
par arrest de la Court fut dict
(*dit*) que, C; 64.
cette *diversité* est par trop grande,
que, S, X; 32.
c'est *dommage* dont, I; 53.
être *dommage* que, I, S, X; 53.
[quel *dommage* que, S, France]; 53.

pouvoir s'*émerveiller* que, I; 45.
n. s'*émerveiller* que, S; 50.
s'*émerveiller* de ce que, I; 45, 46.
[s'*émerveiller* qui, I]; 44.
[s'*émerveiller* si, X]; cf. s'ébahir si.
empêcher que, I, S, X, [S, France];
   55, 56, 69, 70.
n. *empêcher* que, S, X; 60.
n. pouvoir *empêcher* que, S, X,
   [S, France]; 60.
il seroit bien *employé* que, S; 76.
[s'*encliner* à ce que, S]; 61.
[*encor* (with inversion), S]; 121.
encore où, I; 121, 122.
encore que, I, C, S, X; 121-124, 128.
endurer que, S, X; 61.
? *endurer* que, S, X; 62.
n. *endurer* que, S; 62.
n. pouvoir *endurer* que, S, X; 62.
engarder que, S; 56.
enjoindre que, S; 56.
[*ennuyer* à qlqn que]; 46.
[*ennuyer* à qlqn que (vol), S]; 77.
[*enorter* que, I, C]; 7.
[*enorter* que (vol), S, X]; 56.
[n. pouvoir *enorter* que, S]; 60.
enragé que; 46, 47.
enseigner que, I, X, [I, France]; 7.
[n. *enseigner* que (vol), S]; 60.
prendre *enseignes* (avec qlqn) que,
   S; 64.
ensi: see also ainsi.
[*ensi* com (comparative), I, F]; 104.
[*ensi* que (result), I]; 92.
s'*ensuivre* que, S; 31, 72.
s'*ensuivre* que, I, F, C, X; 31, 41.
n. s'*ensuivre* que, S; 37.
entant que, I, X; 117.
mettre en l'*entendement* de qlqn que
   (p. si), S; 26.
entendre comment, [I], I; 131.
entendre que, [I, X], I, F, C, X,
   [I, France]; 7.

entendre que (p. si), I, X; 25.
n. *entendre* que, I, S, X; 9.
n. ? *entendre* que, I; 22.
entendre que (vol), S, X; 59.
n. *entendre* que (vol), S; 60.
faire *entendre* que, [I, C], I, X, [I,
   France]; 7.
faire *entendre* que (vol), S; 59.
[pouvoir *entendre* que (p. si), S]; 25.
n. pouvoir *entendre* que, X; 9.
donner à *entendre* que, donner
   entendre que, [I], I, F, X; 7.
entendre et vouloir que, S; 59.
[en celle *entente* que, sus celle
   entente et volenté que, C, X]; 55,
   63, 64.
[*entrues* que, I]; 113.
avoir *envie* que, S, X; 59.
n. *épargner* que, S; 101.
éprouver que, I; 7.
éprouver si, [II], I; 134.
es-: see also é-.
[suen *escient*, I]; cf. que je sache,
   139.
[*esgarder* que, X]; 56.
[*esgarder* (juger) que, I]; 7.
[s'*esmaiier* que]; 46.
est une chose non moins *esmerveilla-*
   ble que notable, que, I; 32.
avoir *espérance* que, F, C, S, X; 5.
? avoir *espérance* que, S; 22.
[n. avoir *espérance* que, S]; 13.
y avoir *espérance* (par nous) que,
   C; 7.
[donner *espérance* que, C]; 7.
(être) en *espérance* que, X; 7.
non sans *espérance* que, F; 7.
sous *espérance* que, C; 7.
espérer que, [F, C, S], F, C, S, X; 4.
n. *espérer* que, S, X; 12.
non par *espoir* que, X; 13.
sans *espoir* que, S, X; 13.
[être en bon *espoir* que, S]; 5.

mais que, [S, X], S, X, [S, France]; 110, *RR* 15.

[ne *mais* que, S]; *RR* 15.

n. pouvoir être *maîtresse* de qlch qu'il ne, X; 101.

il n'y a point de *mal* que, S; 78.

le *mal* est que, le mal fut que, I, X; 32.

[tourner à *mal* que (personal subject), X]; 61, 69, cf. 32, cf. 55.

être *malaisé* que, S; 35.

malgré que (e.g., malgré qu'il en eust), X; 125.

être un *malheur* que, S; 53.

[être *malheureux* que (personal subject)]; 46.

mander que, [I, F, C, X], I, C, [F, France]; 7.

mander que (vol), [S, X], S, X; 59.

sans *mander* que, S; 11, 20.

n. *mander* que, I, X; 11.

de *manière* que (result), I, C, SC, X; 92.

de *manière* que (purpose), S, X; 88.

en *manière* que (result), I, X; 92.

[en telle *manière* que (result), I, F]; 92.

[en telle *manière* que (purpose), S]; 88.

par telle *manière* que (result), [I], C; 92.

[par telle *manière* que (purpose), S, X]; 88.

être *manifeste* que, I, X; 31.

mar; 66, 135.

n. être *marri* dont (personal subject), X; 45, 46, 48.

être *marri* que, I, S, X; 46, 47.

être *marri* de ce que; 45, 46.

trouver *mauvais* que, I, S, X; 61, 69.

n. trouver *mauvais* que, S, X; 62.

trouver *mauvais* de ce que; 46.

c'est une chose *mauvaise* que, I; 32.

se *mécontenter* de quoi, I; 45, 46.

être le *meilleur* pour qlqn qu'il, S; 78.

le *meilleur* que, [I, S, SC], F, S, X; *PQ* 9-15.

le *meilleur* qui, [S], S; *PQ* 9-15.

[le *meilleur* . . . (noun) . . . comme, I]; *PQ* 9-15.

le *meilleur* . . . (noun) . . . dont, I; *PQ* 9-15.

le *meilleur* . . . (noun) . . . d'où, C; *PQ* 9-15.

le *meilleur* . . . (noun) . . . que (accusative), [S, X], I, F, C, S, X; *PQ* 9-15.

le *meilleur* . . . (noun) . . . que (conjunction), I, X; *PQ* 9-15.

le *meilleur* . . . (noun) . . . qui, [S], I, S, X, [S, France]; *PQ* 9-15.

mêmement que, I; 117.

avoir *memoire* que, I; 7.

[il n'est point en *memoire* que, S]; 37.

menacer que, F, C; 7.

s'estimer *méprisé* que, X; 46, cf. 45.

[en *mercier* qlqn qu'il, I]; 117.

meriter que, S, X; 61.

meriter que (p. si), X; 62.

n. *meriter* que, S; 62.

[avoir *merveille* comment, C]; 44, 131.

[avoir *merveille* que, X]; 44, 45.

est *merveille* comme, c'est merveille comme, [X], I; 131.

[être *merveille* comment, I]; 131.

être *merveille* que, [I, X], I, X; 53.

n. être *merveille* si, [I], I; cf. 45.

[tenir à *merveille* que, X]; cf. 32.

[venir à *merveille* à qlqn que, I]; 45.

[se *merveiller* que (ce que), I]; 44.

[avoir *mestier* que (personal subject), X]; 61.

n. être *mestier* que, [S], X; 72.

le *plus* . . . (adj. noun) . . . que (conjunction), I, F, C, X; *PQ* 9-15.

le *plus* . . . (adj. noun) . . . qui, [I, S], I, C, S, X, [S, France]; *PQ* 9-15.

plus omitted: Pasquier, lun des grands gaudisseurs qui soit dicy à la journée dun cheval (Fail).

[le *plus* . . . (adv.) . . . comme, X]; *see* comme (comparative).

le *plus* . . . (adv.) . . . que, [I, F, S], I, F, C, S, SC, X, [F, France]; *PQ* 9-15.

plustost que, plus tost que: *see* tôt.

porter que, I; 7.

n. *porter* que, S; 11.

porter (comporter) que, I, X; 101.

porter (comporter) que (p. si), X; 101.

posé que, [S], X; *RR* 15.

cela étant *posé*, que, I; *RR* 15.

poser que, S, X; 2.

? *poser* que, S; 22.

possible que; 34.

possible (modal adv.): possible ne se trouverent pas viandes prestes (Desp.).

être *possible* que (p. si), X; 40.

? être *possible* que, I, S, X; 38.

demander comment il est *possible* que, S; 34.

n. être *possible* que, S, X; 37.

n. ? être *possible* que, S; 39.

n. voir comment il est *possible* que, S; 37.

pour; 85, 126; *see also* prou–.

pour que; 34, 84-86, 111.

ce n'est pas un motif *pour* que; 85.

pour que (pourvu que, si); 85.

pour . . . (adj.) . . . que, S; 125.

pour . . . (adv.) . . . que; 126.

pour . . . (noun) . . . que, [I, S, X], I, S, X; 125, 126.

pour . . . (noun) . . . qui, [S], S, X; 125.

pour ce (afin) que; 84-86.

pour ce que, pour çou que, por ce que, pource que, [I, C, SC, X], I, C, X; 85, 117, 126.

non *pour* ce que, non pour çou que, non pource que, [S, X], X; 118.

[non pas *pour* çou que, S]; 118.

pour peu que, S, X, [S, France]; 125.

pour si peu . . . (adj.) . . . que, S; 125.

pour quoi, pourquoi, pour que; 126, cf. 85.

[se *pourpenser* que, C]; 7.

pourquoi (in indirect interrogation); 131, 132.

[*pour* tant que, I, SC, X]; 117.

pour autant que, I; 117.

pourtant que, I, X; 117.

[*pourvoir* à ce que, S, France]; 55, 56.

pourvu que, S, X; 85, *PQ* 15.

n. *pouvoir* que, X; 101.

[se *pouvoir* que (impersonal), S, France]; 34.

[? se *pouvoir* que (impersonal), S, France]; 38.

n. se *pouvoir* que (impersonal), X; 37.

pratiquer que, X; 56.

prêcher que, I; 7.

predire que, I, F, C; 7.

[*préférer* que, S, France]; 56.

prejuger que, I; 7.

premier que, I, S; 112.

le *premier* que, I, S; *PQ* 16.

le *premier* qui, [I], I, F, X; *PQ* 16.

[le *premier* . . . (noun) . . . dont, S, France]; *PQ* 16.

Q

? être *raisonnable* que, S; 76.

n. être *raisonnable* que, S, X; 76.

être chose *raisonnable* que, X; 76.

n. sembler *raisonnable* à qlqn que, S; 76.

[bien me *ramembre* et me souvient que, I]; 31.

[m'em *ramembre* que, I]; 7.

ramentevoir à qlqn que, I; 7.

n. *ramentevoir* à qlqn que (p. quand) I; 14.

faire *rapport* que, I; 7.

rapporter que, [I], I, [I, France]; 7.

être *ratifié* que, C; 64.

reciter que, I; 7.

[*reclamer* que, S]; 56.

[être *recommandé* que, S]; 56.

recommander que, S, X; 56.

se *reconforter* en ce que, F; 45.

reconnaître que, [I], I, [I, C, X, France]; 7.

reconnaître que (p. si), S, SC; 25.

reconnaître que (p. sinon que), I; 25.

[ouïr *recorder* comment, I]; 131.

[redoter (*redouter*) que (p. n. convenir à qlqn), S]; 46, 50.

[se *redouter* que, X]; 46.

[fut *regardé* et consideré que, S]; *see* consideré.

regarder que, [I, C], I, X; 7.

[n. avoir *regart* que, X]; 101.

[nc. devoir *regehir* que, S]; 19.

c'est une reigle (*règle*) que, I, X; 32.

avec *regret* que, S; 46.

avec *regret* de ce que, X; 45.

avoir *regret* que, I, S, X; 46.

regretter que, I, S, X, [S, France]; 46.

n. *regretter* que, S; 50.

se *réjouir* que, S; 46, 47.

[*relouer* que, S]; 56.

[ne *remandra* (remanoir) que, S]; 72.

remarquer que, I, X, [I, X, France]; 7.

[faire *remarquer* que, I, France]; 7.

donner *remède* que, X; 59.

le *remède* est que, S; 59.

faire *remonstrances* à ce que, S, X; 59.

remonstrer comme, C; 131.

remonstrer que, [I, C], I, F, C, Cc, X; 7.

remonstrer que (vol), [S], S, X; 59.

[courir *renommée* que (impersonal), I]; 31.

[se *repentir* que]; 46, 47.

répéter que, I; 7.

repliquer que (vol), X; 59.

n. ? pouvoir *repliquer* que, I; 22.

répondre que, [I, C], I, F, C, SC, X, [I, France]; 7.

répondre que (vol), [S, X], S, X; 59.

[vouloir *répondre* que (p. si), S]; 27.

avoir *réponse* que, I; 7.

faire *réponse* que, I, C; 7.

faire *réponse* que (vol), S; 59.

representer que, I; 7.

n. *reprocher* que, S; 11.

reprocher à qlqn que, [I, C], I, X; 7.

n. *reprouver* qlqn à ce que, X; 45, cf. 32.

reputer que, Cc; 7.

requerir que, [S, X], S, X; 56.

n. vouloir *requerir* que, S; 60.

faire *requeste* que, [S], S; 59.

présenter *requête* que, S; 59.

être *requis* que, [S], S, X; 56.

il avoit été *resolu* que, C; 64.

il n'étoit pas encore *résolu* si, C; 134.

être *resolu* en persuasion que (personal subject), I; 7.

la *résolution* s'est prise que, F; 64.

estoit sa *resolution* qu'il, C; 7, 64.

se *résoudre* que, I; 7.

se *résoudre* que (vol), X; 64.

n. pouvoir *resoudre* en son entendement que, X; 10.

n. pouvoir *résoudre* qlqn que, S; 10, cf. 64, 67.
rester que (impersonal), S; 72.
il *reste* (que), S, X; 72.
n. *rester* que (impersonal), S; 37.
[*résulter* que, I, X, France]; 31.
[a grant painne se *retarde* . . . quë, X]; 56, 101.
retenir que, S, X; 56.
n. pouvoir *retenir* qlqn que, S; 60.
c'est grand *richesse* que, S; 78.
[être *ridicule* que, S, France]; 32, 53.
n. falloir estimer comme *rien*, que, I; 32.
[*rover* que, S, X]; 56.

S

(jamais) que je *sache;* 139.
estimer *sain* que, X; 61.
sans que, [S], S, X, [X, France]; 36, 98, 111, *RR* 15.
sans ce que, [I, S, X], I, S, X; 98, 111, *RR* 15.
sans cela que, I; *RR* 15.
à grant peine se peürent-ilz *saulver* que, S; 101.
sauver qlqn que, S; 56.
sauver qlch à ce que, X; 56.
savoir comme, I, X; 131.
? *savoir* comme, I; 131.
n. *savoir* comme, X; 132, cf. 54 (Gaut.).
[*savoir* comment, I]; 131.
n. *savoir* comment, [I, S], C; 132.
[n. pouvoir *savoir* comment, S]; 132.
n. *savoir* dire quel, lequel, [I, SC], I, X; 132.
savoir que, [I, F, C, SC, X], I, F, C, Cc, S, SC, X, [I, F, C, X, France]; 1, 46.
[*savoir* (que), I]; 1.
savoir que (p. si), [S, X], I; 24.
[*savoir* que (p. ne mais que), S]; 24.

n. *savoir* que, [S], I, S, X, [I, France]; 8, 16.
n. ? *savoir* que, I, F, C, X; 22.
[*savoir* que (ce que), I]; 131.
? *savoir* que (ce que), [I], I; 131.
n. *savoir* que (ce que), [I, C, S, SC, X], I, F; 34, 132.
savoir ce que, I; 131.
n. *savoir* ce que, F; 132.
desavouer *savoir* que, X; 1, 19.
[faire *savoir* que, I, France]; 1.
faire *savoir* que (vol), S, X; 59.
n. *savoir* quel, I; 132.
n. *savoir* quel . . . (noun), [I, X], I, F, C; 132.
[*savoir* qui, I]; 131.
n. *savoir* qui, [I], I; 132.
n. *savoir* ce qui, I, F; 132.
n. *savoir* quoi, S; 132.
savoir si, [I, F, C, SC], I, F, SC, [I, France]; 134.
n. *savoir* si, [I, S], I, F, C, SC, X; 134.
être *scandalisé* de ce que; 45, 46.
selon que, I, F, C; 104.
faire *semblant* que, I; 7.
n. faire *semblant* que, [S], X; 11.
[montrer *semblant* que, I]; 7.
sembler que; 33, 41.
n. *sembler* que, S, SC, X; 37.
sembler à qlqn que; 33, 41.
sembler à qlqn que (vol), I (doibvoit), S; 77.
sembler à qlqn que (p. si), S, X; 40.
? *sembler* à qlqn que, S, SCc; 38.
n. *sembler* à qlqn que, S, X; 37.
n. ? *sembler* à qlqn que, S; 39.
[ce *semblait* . . . (noun) . . . qui, S]; 33, *PQ* 2 (note 3).
semer que, I, C; 7.
[*semondre* que, S, X]; 56.
[tomber sous le *sens* que, C, France]; 31.
sentir que, [I, C, X], I, X; 7.

[*sentir* que (p. si), S]; 25.
n. *sentir* que, I; 14.
se *sentir* que, X; 7.
[*seoir* à qlqn que, S]; 77.
faire *serment* que, C; 7.
[le *seul* que, X, France]; *PQ* 16.
[le *seul* qui, S, France]; *PQ* 16.
[un *seul* qui, I, C]; *PQ* 16.
le *seul* . . . (noun) . . . que, S, X, [X,
   France]; *PQ* 16.
le *seul* . . . (noun) . . . qui, I, [S,
   France]; *PQ* 16.
n'est pas ceste nation *seulle* à qui, I;
   PQ 16.
le *seul* . . . (noun) . . . par lequel, I,
   X; *PQ* 16.
si; 85, 124, *RR* 12.
si (concessive); 124.
si (implying interrogation); 134.
si . . . (adj.) . . . que (concessive),
   S, [S, France]; 125.
si . . . (adj.) . . . que (result), [I, F,
   C, SC, X], I, F, C, S, SC, X, [I,
   X, France]; 94.
si . . . (adj.) . . . que (result) (p.
   quand), S; 100.
si . . . (adj.) . . . que (result) (p. si),
   S; 100.
? *si* . . . (adj.) . . . que (result), [SC],
   S, X; 99.
n. *si* . . . (adj.) . . . que (result), [S,
   SC, X], I, S, X; 96, 106-108.
[n. *si* . . . (adj.) . . . (que) (result),
   X]; 96.
si . . . (adj.) . . . que (purpose), [S,
   X], S, X; 90.
[*si* . . . (adj.) . . . que (comparative),
   C]; 104.
n. *si* . . . (adj.) . . . qui (result),
   [Cc, S, X], S; *PQ* 17.
si . . . (adv.) . . . que (result), [I, F,
   C, SC, X], I, F, C, S, SC, X, [I,
   France]; 94, cf. 34 (Vaugelas).

si . . . (adv.) . . . que (result) (p. si),
   I; 100.
n. *si* . . . (adv.) . . . que . . . (affirmative clause), S, X; 96, 106, 107.
n. *si* . . . (adv.) . . . que . . . (negative clause), [S, SC, X], S, SC, X;
   96, 106-108.
si . . . (adv.) . . que (purpose), [S],
   S, X; 90.
[*si* . . . (verb) . . . que (result), I, F,
   C, X]; 94.
[n. *si* . . . (verb) . . . que . . . (negative clause), S]; 96.
[*si* . . . (verb) . . . que (purpose),
   S]; 90.
si bien que (result) (conclusive), [I],
   I, F, C, SC, X; 92, 93, 102.
[*si* com, si come, si comme, sicomme,
   I, F]; 104.
[*si* com (temporal), I]; 110.
[*si* comme (comparative), I]; 104.
comme *si*, [I, S, X], I, S, X, [I, S,
   France]; *RR* 13.
tel que *si*, I, S; *RR* 13.
si que (result) (conclusive), [I, F,
   SC, X], I, F, X; 83, 92, 93.
? *si* que (result) (conclusive), S; 99.
si que (purpose), [S], S; 88.
[*si* que (comparative), I]; 104.
[par *si* que, S, X]; *RR* 15.
par tel *si* que, F; *RR* 15.
[*sifait* . . . (noun) . . ., C]; 94.
signe que, C; 7.
n. y avoir plus grand *signe* que, S;
   13.
être *signe* que, I, X; 7.
faire *signe* que, I; 7.
faire *signe* que (vol), S, X; 59.
signifier que, I, C; 7.
n. ? vouloir *signifier* que, I; 22.
sinon: si . . . non (si ce n'est) [teus
   n'a onques se mal non (Gaut.,
   3714)].

sinon que (sans ce que), I; *RR* 14.
sinon que (excepté que), [I], I, X, [I, France]; *RR* 14.
sinon que (si . . . ne), [S], S, X; *RR* 14.
sitôt que, F; 109.
avoir le *soin* que, S; 59.
soit (concessive); 125.
soit que, S, X; 125.
comme ainsi *soit* que: *see* comme.
solliciter que, S, X; 56.
songer que, I, X, [I, France]; 2.
n. *songer* que, X, [I, France]; 10.
faire *songer* que, I; 2, 7.
se *songer* que, I, Cc, X; 7.
de *sorte* que (result) (conclusive), I, F, Fc, C, X; 92, 93, 102.
de *sorte* que (result) (p. si), S; 100.
de telle *sorte* que (result), I, F, C, X; 92.
en *sorte* que (result) (conclusive), I, F, C, SC, X, [I, France]; 92.
? en *sorte* que (result) (conclusive), S; 99.
en *sorte* que (purpose), S, X; 88.
en telle *sorte* que (result), I, F, C, X; 92.
faire en *sorte* que (result), F; 55.
faire en *sorte* que (purpose), S; 55.
? se *soucier* que, S; 51.
n. se *soucier* que, S; 50.
n. se *soucier* qui, C, S; 133.
souffrir que, [I], S, X; 61.
n. *souffrir* que, [S], S, X, [S, France]; 62.
n. falloir *souffrir* que, X; 62.
pouvoir *souffrir* que, X; 61.
n. pouvoir *souffrir* que, X; 62.
n. vouloir *souffrir* que, S, X; 62.
[pouvoir *soufire* (suffire) que (p. si), S]; 74.
souhaiter que, [X], S, X, [S, France]; 56.

[sur le *soupçon* que, I, France]; 7.
avoir *soupçon* que, X; 2.
soupçonner que, I, S, X; 2.
n. *soupçonner* que, X; 10.
[sans laisser *soupçonner* que, I, France]; 19.
n. pouvoir *soupçonner* que, X; 10.
[*soupirer* que, I, France]; 7.
soutenir que, [I], I, C, [I, France]; 7.
nc. vouloir *soutenir* que, X; 20.
souvenir à qlqn que (impersonal), [I], I, X; 31.
n. *souvenir* à qlqn que (impersonal), S; 37.
n.? *souvenir* à qlqn que (impersonal), I; 39.
faire *souvenir* à qlqn que, I; 7.
se *souvenir* que, I; 7.
n. se *souvenir* que, X; 11.
[*spécifier* que, I, France]; 7.
suffire que, I, S, X; 74.
[n. juger *superflu* que, X, France]; 62.
supplier que, [S], I, C, S, X; 55-57.
supplier à ce que, S; 55, 56.
? *supporter* que, X; 62.
supposer que, [I, F, C], [I, France]; 2.
[la *supposition* est que, X]; 5.
être *sûr* (seurs, seür, seur, sceur) que, [F], I, F, C, SC; 7.
[n. être assez *sûr* que, X, France]; 10.
le plus *sûr* était que, S; 78.
se tenir *sûr* que, C; 7.
se tenir comme *sûr* que, C; 7.
engendre *suspection* que, X; 5.
être en *suspicion* que, S, X; 5.
éviter *suspicion* que, X; 19.
mettre en *suspicion* que, I; 5.

T

tâcher (tascher) que, X; 56.
[n. avoir *talant* que, X]; 59.
[*talanz* li prant quë, S]; 77.
[venir à qlqn *talanz* que, S]; 77.
tandis que (tant que), I, F; 110.
tandis que, I, C, [I, France]; 110.
tant (concessive), [S], S, X; 125.
[*tant* com om une piere rue (comparative)]; 104.
[*tant* comme (with past time), I]; 110.
tant comme (with present or future time), [I, F, S, X], F; 110.
[*tant* comme (comparative), I, X]; 104.
tant (d'autant) plus que, I; 117.
tant que (with past time), [I, C, S], I, C, SC, X; 110.
tant que (with present or future time), [I, F, S, X], I, F, C, S, X, [F, France]; 110.
tant que (comparative), I, F, C, X; 104.
tant (jusqu'à ce) que (with past time), [I, C, S, X], I, X; 113.
tant (jusqu'à ce) que (with present or future time), [I, F, S, X], F, S; 113.
tant que, tant . . . que, (result), [I, F, SC, X], I, F, C, SC, X; 94.
[*tant* que, tant . . . que, (result) (p. si), S, X]; 100.
n. *tant* que, tant . . . que, (result), [S, X], S, X; 97.
tant . . . que (purpose), [S], X; 90.
n. ? *tant* . . . que (purpose), S; 90.
tant . . . (adj.) . . . que (result), [I, C, SC, X], I, F, C, SC, X; 94.
tant . . . (adj.) . . . que (result) (p. combien que), S; 100.
tant . . . (adj.) . . . que (result) (p. si), C, X; 100.

? *tant* . . . (adj.) . . . que (result), X; 99.
n. *tant* . . . (adj.) . . . que (result), [S, X], SC, X; 97.
tant . . . (adj.) . . . que (purpose), S; 90.
tant . . . (adv.) . . . que (result), I, F, X; 94.
[*tant* . . . (noun) . . . que (result), I]; 94.
tant . . (verb) . . . que (result), [I, X], I, F, C, SC, X, [I, France]; 94.
tant . . . (verb) . . . que (result) (p. si), [S], X; 100.
tant . . . (verb) . . . que (result) (p. ? si), S; 99, 100.
n. *tant* . . . (verb) . . . que (result), [S], S, SC, X; 97.
tant . . . (verb) . . . que (purpose), [S], S; 90.
tant (duration) . . . (verb) . . . que (result), [I, SC], I, X; 94.
tant (duration) . . . (verb) . . . que (result) (conclusive), I; 94.
[n. *tant* (duration) . . . (verb) . . . que (result), S]; 97.
tant y a que, I, Fc, C, SC, X; 31, 94.
si *tant* est que, était que, S; 40.
en *tant* que, I; 117, cf. entant que.
faire *tant* que (result), [I, F], I, X; 94.
[faire *tant* que (result) (p. si), S]; 100.
[n. pouvoir faire *tant* que (result), X]; 97.
faire *tant* que (purpose), [S, X], S; 90, 92.
[par *tant* que, I]; 117.
[être tart (*tard*) à qlqn que, S]; 77.
[sembler tart (*tard*) à qlqn que, X]; 77.
[n. *tarder* que (impersonal), I]; 113.

toutefois que, toutesfois que, I, S; 121.

c'est fraude et *trahison* que: *see* fraude.

traiter que, [S], S; 56.

se *traiter* que, C; 64.

travailler que, S; 56.

[*tresque*, S]; 113.

se *troubler* de ce que, X; 45.

trouver (découvrir) que, [I], I, F, C, X; 7.

n. *trouver* (découvrir) que, S, X; 9.

n. *trouver* (découvrir) que (p. si), X; 25.

trouver (estimer, juger) que, I, Cc, X, [I, France]; 7.

? *trouver* (estimer, juger) que, X; 21.

n. *trouver* (estimer, juger) que, S, X; 10.

trouver . . . (adj.) . . . que: *see* the adj.

se *trouver* que, I; 31, 41.

U

[avoir *usage* que, X]; 32.

être en *usance* que (impersonal), X; 32.

être *utile* que (p. combien que), S; 75.

utinam; 135.

V

c'est en *vain* que, X; 32.

valoir que, S, X; 61.

n. *valoir* que, S; 62.

valoir autant que (hypothetical comparison: autant vauldroit que je le tinse desjà); cf. 78.

valoir mieux que (impersonal), S, X, [S, France]; 78.

valoir mieux que (impersonal) (p. si), X; 78.

[*valoir* mieux à qlqn qu'il, S]; 78.

[n. *valoir* qlch à qlqn qu'il ne, X]; 78.

se *vanter* que, [C], I, F, C; 7.

[*veiller* à ce que, S, France]; 56.

venir que (impersonal), [I], I, C, X; 31, 41.

venir son jour qu'il (p. si), S; *RR* 6.

[*venir* à qlqn qu'il (impersonal), X]; 31, 41.

[*venir* mieux à qlqn qu'il S, X]; 78.

bien est *veriforme* que, I; 33.

est chose *veritable* que, SCc; 31.

c'est chose *tresveritable* que, I; 31.

la *vérité* est que, fut que, [I], I; 31.

réputer cela être un grand *vice* que, I; 32.

c'est force et *violence* que: *see* force.

[être *vis* à qlqn que, I, S, X]; 33.

[exprimer le *vœu* que, S, France]; 59.

faire *vœu* que, F; 7.

n. *voir* comment, [X], I, S; 132.

n. *voir* pourquoi, S, Sc; 132.

voir que (vol), [S], S; 61.

voir que, [I, F, C, X], I, F, C, X, [I, France]; 9.

voir que (p. si), [S], S, X; 25.

voir que (p. sinon que), S; 25.

? *voir* que, S, X; 21, 22.

n. *voir* que, Ic, S, X; 9, 10.

[n. *voir* que (p. si), I]; 9, 25.

n. ? *voir* que, I, F, C, X; 22.

n. *voir* par quel moyen, S; 132.

être aisé à *voir* que, I; 7.

il fait beau *voir* que, S; 6.

s'étonner *voir* que, I; 7, 46.

se *voir* que, I; 31.

[mes *volantez* an moi s'aüne, que, S]; 77.

[sus celle entente et *volenté* que, C]; 63, 64.

volition (with que, in Commynes and later authors), S, X, [S, X, France]; 136, 137.

BIBLIOGRAPHY

GRAMMARIANS AND PHILOLOGISTS

[ANONYMOUS], Un Petit Livre pour enseigner les enfantz de leur entreparler comun francois. Early 15th century. E. Stengel in Zeitschrift für neufranzösische Sprache und Literatur, I, 1879.

AUGÉ, CLAUDE, Grammaire, cours supérieur, livre du maître, conforme à la nouvelle nomenclature grammaticale. Paris, Larousse, 1922.

AYER, C. [NICOLAS-LOUIS-CYPRIEN], Grammaire comparée de la langue française, 4e édition. Paris, 1885.

BARTON, JOHN, Donait francois pour briefment entroduyr les Anglois en la droit language du Paris et de pais la d'entour fait aus despenses de Johan Barton par pluseurs bons clerc du language avandite. Ca. 1400. E. Stengel in Zeitschrift für neufranzösische Sprache und Literatur, I, 1879.

BEHRENS, see Schwan.

BENOIST, ANTOINE, De la syntaxe française entre Palsgrave et Vaugelas. Paris, E. Thorin, 1877.

BOURCIEZ, ÉDOUARD, Éléments de linguistique romane, 2e édition. Paris, 1923.

BRUNOT, FERDINAND, Précis de grammaire historique de la langue française, 3e édition. Paris, 1894.

——Histoire de la langue française des origines à 1900. Paris, 1905-1933.

——La Pensée et la langue, 2e édition. Paris, Masson, 1922.

CHASSANG, see Vaugelas.

CLÉDAT, L., Grammaire historique du français. Paris, Garnier Frères, 1889.

DARMESTETER, ARSÈNE, Cours de grammaire historique de la langue française. Paris, Delagrave, 1895.

—— AND HATZFELD, ADOLPHE, Le Seizième Siècle en France. Paris, Delagrave, 1889.

DESMARAIS, FRANÇOIS-SERAPHIN RÉGNIER, Traité de la grammaire françoise (initiated by the French Academy). Bruxelles, Eugene Henry Fricx, 1706.

161

DONATUS, AELIUS, Methodis grammatices, Donato authore. Argentinae, apud J. Knoblouchium, 1522.

DUBOIS, JACQUES (JACOBI SYLVII . . .), In lingvam gallicam isagωge, vna cum ejusdem grammatica latino-gallica, ex hebræis, græcis, & latinis authoribus. Parisiis ex officina Roberti Stephani, 1531.

DU GUEZ, GILES, An Introductorie for to lerne to rede, to pronounce and to speke French trewly, compyled for . . . the Lady Mary of Englande, doughter to . . . Kyng Henry the Eight. London [1532]. *See* Génin.

ESTIENNE, ROBERT, De Gallica verborum declinatione. Parisiis, ex officina Rob. Stephani, 1540.

——Traicte de la grãmaire francoise. Paris, 1569 (completed 1558).

ÉTIENNE, EUGÈNE, Essai de grammaire de l'ancien français (IXᵉ-XIVᵉ siècles). Paris et Nancy, 1895.

FOULET, LUCIEN, Petite Syntaxe de l'ancien français, 2ᵉ édition. Paris, Champion, 1923.

GARNIER, JEAN, Institutio gallicæ linguæ . . . . Genevæ, apud J. Crispinum, 1558.

GÉNIN, F., Reprint of the works of Giles du Guez and John Palsgrave, in Collection des documents inédits sur l'histoire de France. Paris, Imprimerie Nationale, 1852.

HAASE, A., Syntaxe française du XVIIᵉ siècle (1898). Traduction par M. Obert. Paris, 1914.

HARRIS, JAMES, AND THUROT, FRANÇOIS, Hermès ou recherches philosophiques sur la grammaire universelle, ouvrage traduit de l'anglois, de Jacques Harris [1752], avec des remarques et des additions, par François Thurot. Paris, Imprimerie de la République, 1796.

HATZFELD, *see* Darmesteter.

HUGUET, EDMOND, Étude sur la syntaxe de Rabelais comparée à celle des autres prosateurs de 1450 à 1550 (thèse de Paris). Paris, Hachette, 1894.

LAMB, WILLIAM W., The Syntax of the Heptameron (dissertation, New York University). New York, 1914.

LA RAMÉE, PIERRE DE, Gramere. Unsigned. Paris, André Wechel, 1562.

——Grammaire. Paris, André Wechel, 1572.

LERCH, EUGEN, Historische französische Syntax. Leipzig, Reisland, 1925, 1929.

LIVET, CHARLES-LOUIS, La Grammaire française et les grammairiens du XVIᵉ siècle. Paris, 1859.

MAUPAS, CHARLES, Grammaire et syntaxe françoise (third edition of Grammaire françoise. Bloys, Philippes Cottereau, 1607). Paris, A. Bacot, 1625 (signed at Blois, 1618).

MEIGRET, LOUIS, Le Tretté de la grammẹre francoẹze. Paris, Chrestien Wechel, 1550.

MELLERIO, L., Lexique de Ronsard précédé d'une étude sur son vocabulaire, son orthographe et sa syntaxe. Paris, Bibliothèque elzévirienne, 1895.

MÉNAGE, GILLES, Observations svr la langve françoise. Paris, Clavde Barbin, 1672.

MEURIER, GABRIEL, Conjugaisons, regles et instructions ... pour ceux qui desirent apprendre françois, italien, espagnol, et flamen .... Anvers, Jan van Vræsberghe, 1558.

MEYER-LÜBKE, W., Grammaire des langues romanes. Traduction par A. et G. Doutrepont. Paris, 1895.

NYROP, KRISTOFFER, Grammaire historique de la langue française. Copenhague, 1899-1925.

OUDIN, ANTOINE, Grammaire françoise rapportée au langage du temps ..., seconde édition. Paris, A. de Sommaville, 1640 (first edition, 1632).

PALSGRAVE, JOHN, Lesclarcissement de la langue francoyse. London, 1530. *See* Génin.

PILLOT, JEAN, Gallicæ linguæ institutio. ... Parisiis, apud Stephanum Groulleau, 1561 (first edition, 1550).

RÉGNIER, ADOLPHE (fils), Lexique de la langue de Malherbe avec une introduction grammaticale. *In* Les Grands Écrivains de la France, V. Paris, Hachette, 1869.

RÉGNIER-DESMARAIS, *see* Desmarais.

RESTAUT, PIERRE, Principes généraux et raisonnés de la grammaire françoise. Paris, Dufart, 1798 (first edition, 1745).

RITCHIE, R. L. GRAEME, Recherches sur la syntaxe de la conjonction «que» dans l'ancien français (thèse de Paris). Paris, Champion, 1907.

RÜBNER, RUDOLPH, Syntaktische Studien zu Bonaventure des Périers (dissertation). Leipzig, 1896.

Scaliger, Jules-César, De Causis linguæ latinæ libri tredecim. In Bibliopolio Commeliniano, 1609 (reprint of the original, 1540).

Schwan, Eduard, and Behrens, Dietrich, Grammaire de l'ancien français. Traduction par Oscar Bloch. Leipzig, 1923.

Sneyders, *see* Vogel.

Soltmann, Hermann, Syntax der Modi im modernen französisch. Halle, 1914.

Thurot, *see* Harris.

Tobler, Adolf, Vermischte Beitrage zur französischen Grammatik. Leipzig, 1908.

Vaugelas, Claude Favre de, Remarques sur la langue françoise. Paris, Veuve Jean Camusat et Pierre le Petit, 1647.

——Remarques sur la langue françoise par Vaugelas. Nouvelle édition . . . par A. Chassang. Versailles et Paris, 1880.

Vogel, K. Sneyders de, Syntaxe historique du français. 2e édition. Groningue, La Haye, J.–B. Wolters, 1927.

Voizard, Eugène, Étude sur la langue de Montaigne. Paris, Léopold Cerf, 1885.

Wailly, Noël-François de, Principes généraux et particuliers de la langue française. Paris, J. Barbou, 1800 (first edition, 1763).

Note—A less specialized bibliography may be consulted in the Bibliographical Aids listed below. A comprehensive bibliography of rhetoric and poetic during the period 1328-1630, together with a bibliography of the classical, medieval, and Italian sources of French poetic theory, may be consulted in Dr. Warner F. Patterson's *Three Centuries of French Poetic Theory, 1328-1630*, forthcoming in this series.

AUTHORS
(Arranged chronologically)

Gautier d'Arras, Eracle. E. Löseth in Bibliothèque française du moyen âge (Œuvres de Gautier d'Arras, Tome Ier). Paris, Émile Bouillon, 1890.

Manuscripts A: Paris, Bibl. Nat. 1444 (anc. 7534); B: Paris, Bibl. Nat. 24430 (anc. Sorbonne 454); T: Turin, Bibl. Naz. L. 1. 13.

Entire work employed: (lines 1-6593).

References indicate lines.

CHRÉTIEN DE TROYES, Cligés. Wendelin Foerster. Halle, Max Niemeyer, 1921.
Manuscripts A: Paris 794; B: Paris 1450; C: Paris 12560; M: Tours; O: Oxford; P: Paris 375; R: Paris 1420; S: Paris 1374; T: Turin.
Entire work employed: (lines 1-6784).
References indicate lines.

FROISSART, JEAN, Chroniques. K. de Lettenhove. Bruxelles, Victor Devaux, 1867.
Volume II: four drafts (1, Amiens; 2, dedicated to Robert de Namurs; 3, bearing special prologue; 4, Rome); XV: single draft.
Portion employed: II, 1-148; XV, 149-300.
References indicate volume and page.

COMMYNES, PHILIPPE DE, Mémoires. J. Calmette. Paris, Champion, 1924.
Based on Dobrée MS, Nantes, probably before 1524.
Manuscripts A: Bibl. Nat., ms. fr. 10156, 1515-1547; B: Bibl. Nat., ms. fr. 3879, 1525-1550; M: ms. Montmorency-Luxembourg, 1500-1550; P: ms. Polignac, *ca.* 1530.
Entire work employed: (I, 1-252; II, 1-341).
References indicate volume and page.

MARGUERITE D'ANGOULÊME, L'Heptaméron des nouvelles. Frédéric Dillaye. Paris, Alphonse Lemerre, 1879.
D'après les meilleurs manuscrits, respectant l'orthographe, bien qu'elle ne soit pas toujours uniforme (I, 258).
Manuscripts: Bibl. Nat. (twelve).
Entire work employed: (I, 1-254; II, 1-277; III, 1-230).
References indicate volume and page.

RABELAIS, FRANÇOIS, Gargantua, Pantagruel. Abel Lefranc. Paris, Champion, 1912, 1922.
Based on the edition of F. Juste, Lyon, 1542.
Portion employed: first four volumes (I, 1-214; II, 215-441; III, 3-144; IV, 145-348).
References indicate chapter and line.

DES PÉRIERS, BONAVENTURE, Contes ou nouvelles récréations et joyeux devis, suivis du Cymbalum mundi. P. L. Jacob. Paris, Garnier Frères, 1872.
Based on the edition of Robert Granjon, Lyon, 1558. Pp. 303-332 (Cymbalum mundi), published by Jehan Morin, Paris, 1537.
Portion employed: pp. 5-230, 303-332.
References indicate pages.

CALVIN, JEAN, Institution de la religion chrestienne. Abel Lefranc. Paris, Champion, 1911.
Texte de la première édition française, 1541.
Entire work employed: (pp. XLIII + 822), of which pp. II-XLII, 1-25, 212-319, 753-783 are employed in the text, and the remaining pages, in the Appendix.
References, including capital roman numerals, indicate pages.

—— Œuvres françoises. P. L. Jacob. Paris, Charles Gosselin, 1842.
Based on the edition of C. Badius, Geneva, 1558. Pp. 107-136, published 1549.
Portion employed: pp. 25-105, 107-136.
References indicate pages.

DU FAIL, NOËL, Propos rustiques. Jacques Boulenger in Collection des chefs-d'œuvre méconnus. Paris, Bossard, 1921.
Text of the edition of Jean de Tournes, Lyon, 1547.
Entire work employed (pp. 25-163).
References indicate pages.

—— Contes et discours d'Eutrapel. J. Assézat in Bibliothèque elzévirienne (Œuvres facétieuses de Noël du Fail, Tome II). Paris, Paul Daffis, 1874.
Edition of S. W. Singer, Chiswick, 1815, a reprint of the edition of Estienne Groulleau, Paris, 1548.
Portion employed: pp. 212-319.
References indicate pages of volume mentioned above.

RONSARD, PIERRE DE, Les Amours. P. Laumonnier in Société des textes français modernes (Œuvres complètes de Pierre de Ronsard, Tome IV). Paris, Hachette, 1925.
Based on the edition of Veuve Maurice de la Porte, Paris, 1552.
Entire work employed (pp. 4-179).
References indicate pages of volume mentioned above.

—— La Franciade. P. Blanchemain in Bibliothèque elzévirienne (Œuvres complètes de Pierre de Ronsard, Tome III). Paris, 1858.
Based on the edition of G. Buon, Paris, 1572.
Portion employed: pp. 37-39, 43-137.
References indicate pages of volume mentioned above.

PALISSY, BERNARD, Œuvres complètes. Paul-Antoine Cap. Paris, J.-J. Dubochet, 1844.
Edition of Barthélemy Berton, La Rochelle, 1563.
Portion employed: pp. 3-51, 92-123, 129-182, 337-357.
References indicate pages.

AMYOT, JACQUES, Pericles et Fabius Maximus (Les Vies des hommes illustres grecs et romains). Louis Clément in Société des textes français modernes. Paris, Édouard Cornély, 1906.
Edition of Michel de Vascosan, Paris, 1579.
Entire work employed: (pp. xxvii + 115).
References, including capital roman numerals, indicate pages.

ESTIENNE, HENRI, La Précellence du langage françois. Edmond Huguet. Paris, Armand Colin, 1896.
Edition of Mamert Patisson, Paris, 1579.
Portion employed: pp. 1-201.
References indicate pages.

MONTAIGNE, MICHEL DE, Essais. Pierre Villey. Paris, Félix Alcan, 1922.
Nouvelle édition conforme au texte de l'exemplaire de Bordeaux (edition of Abel Langelier [L'Angelier], Paris, 1588, corrected by the author).
Portion employed: I, 3-99; III, 339-451.
References indicate volume and page.

DU VAIR, GUILLAUME, Actions et traictez oratoires. René Radouant in Société des textes français modernes. Paris, Édouard Cornély, 1911.
Based on the edition of Abel L'Angelier, Paris, 1606. Variants B: edition of 1606; C: edition of 1625; D: edition of 1641.
Entire work employed: (pp. 1-207).
References indicate pages.

MALHERBE, FRANÇOIS DE, Lettres à Peiresc. Ludovic Lalanne in Les Grands Écrivains de la France (Œuvres de Malherbe, Tome III). Paris, Hachette, 1862.
Based on the original letters (1606-10 in the portion employed).
Portion employed: III, 1-202.
References indicate volume and page.

FRANCE, ANATOLE, L'Ile des Pingouins, 95ᵉ édition. Paris, Calmann-Lévy, 1908.
Entire work employed: (pp. xv + 416).
References, including capital roman numerals, indicate pages.

BIBLIOGRAPHICAL AIDS

BRUNOT, FERDINAND, Histoire de la langue française des origines à 1900. Paris, 1906. II, 124, Note 1 (supplements Stengel).

HORLUC, PIERRE, AND MARINET, GEORGES, Bibliographie de la syntaxe du français (1840-1905). Paris, 1908.

LE PETIT, JULES, Bibliographie des principales éditions originales d'écrivains français du XVe au XVIIIe siècle. Paris, Jeanne et Brulon, 1927.

LERCH, EUGEN, Historische französische Syntax. Leipzig, Reisland, 1925, 1929. I, xxiv-xxvi and II, xvii-xviii (selective bibliography, to 1929).

MARINET, *see* Horluc.

STENGEL, E., Chronologisches Verzeichnis französischer Grammatiken vom Ende des 14. bis zum Ausgange des 18. Jahrhunderts nebst Angabe der bisher ermittelten Fundorte derselben. Oppeln, 1890.

UNIVERSITY OF MICHIGAN STUDIES

HUMANISTIC SERIES

General Editors:
JOHN G. WINTER, HENRY A. SANDERS, AND EUGENE S. McCARTNEY

Size, 22.7 × 15.2 cm. 8°. Bound in Cloth.

VOL. I. ROMAN HISTORICAL SOURCES AND INSTITUTIONS. Edited by Henry A. Sanders. (*Out of print.*)

VOL. II. WORD FORMATION IN PROVENÇAL. By Edward L. Adams Pp. xvii + 607. $4.00.

VOL. III. LATIN PHILOLOGY. Edited by C. L. Meader. (*Out of print.*)

Parts Sold Separately in Paper Covers:

Part I. THE USE OF IDEM, IPSE, AND WORDS OF RELATED MEANING. By C. L. Meader. Pp. 1–112. $0.75.

Part II. A STUDY IN LATIN ABSTRACT SUBSTANTIVES. By Manson A. Stewart. Pp. 113–178. $0.40.

Part III. THE USE OF THE ADJECTIVE AS A SUBSTANTIVE IN THE DE RERUM NATURA OF LUCRETIUS. By Frederick T. Swan. (*Out of print.*)

Part IV. AUTOBIOGRAPHIC ELEMENTS IN LATIN INSCRIPTIONS. By Henry H. Armstrong. (*Out of print.*)

VOL. IV. ROMAN HISTORY AND MYTHOLOGY. Edited by Henry A. Sanders. (*Out of print.*)

Parts Sold Separately in Paper Covers:

Part I. STUDIES IN THE LIFE OF HELIOGABALUS. By Orma Fitch Butler. Pp. 1–169. $1.25.

Part II. THE MYTH OF HERCULES AT ROME. By J. G. Winter. (*Out of print.*)

Part III. ROMAN LAW STUDIES IN LIVY. By A. E. Evans. Pp. 275–354. $0.40.

Part IV. REMINISCENCES OF ENNIUS IN SILIUS ITALICUS. By Loura B. Woodruff. (*Out of print.*)

VOL. V. SOURCES OF THE SYNOPTIC GOSPELS. By C. S. Patton. Pp. xiii + 263. $1.30.

Size, 28 × 18.5 cm. 4°.

VOL. VI. ATHENIAN LEKYTHOI WITH OUTLINE DRAWING IN GLAZE VARNISH ON A WHITE GROUND. By Arthur Fairbanks. With 15 plates and 57 illustrations in the text. Pp. viii + 371. $4.00.

Orders should be addressed to The Librarian, University of Michigan,
Ann Arbor, Michigan.

Vol. VII. Athenian Lekythoi with Outline Drawing in Matt Color on a White Ground, and an Appendix. By Arthur Fairbanks. With 41 plates. Pp. x + 275. $3.50.

Vol. VIII. The Old Testament Manuscripts in the Freer Collection. By Henry A. Sanders. With 9 plates. Pp. viii + 357. $3.50.

Parts Sold Separately in Paper Covers:

Part I. The Washington Manuscript of Deuteronomy and Joshua. With 3 folding plates. Pp. vi + 104. $1.25.

Part II. The Washington Manuscript of the Psalms. With 1 single plate and 5 folding plates. Pp. viii + 105–349. $2.00.

Vol. IX. The New Testament Manuscripts in the Freer Collection. By Henry A. Sanders. With 8 plates. Pp. x + 323. $3.50.

Parts Sold Separately in Paper Covers:

Part I. The Washington Manuscript of the Four Gospels. With 5 plates. (*Out of print.*)

Part II. The Washington Manuscript of the Epistles of Paul. With 3 plates. Pp. ix + 251–315. $1.25.

Vol. X. The Coptic Manuscripts in the Freer Collection. By William H. Worrell. With 12 plates. Pp. xxvi + 396. $4.75.

Parts Sold Separately in Paper Covers:

Part I. The Coptic Psalter. The Coptic Text in the Sahidic Dialect, with an Introduction, and with 6 plates showing pages of the Manuscript and Fragments in Fasimile. Pp. xxvi + 112. $2.00.

Part II. A Homily on the Archangel Gabriel by Celestinus, Bishop of Rome, and a Homily on the Virgin by Theophilus, Archbishop of Alexandria, from Manuscript Fragments in the Freer Collection and the British Museum. The Coptic Text with an Introduction and Translation, and with 6 plates showing pages of the Manuscripts in facsimile. Pp. 113–396. $2.50.

Vol. XI. Contributions to the History of Science. By Louis C. Karpinski and John G. Winter. With 11 plates. Pp. xi + 283. $3.50.

Parts Sold Separately:

Part I. Robert of Chester's Latin Translation of the Algebra of Al-Khowarizmi. With an Introduction, Critical Notes, and an English Version. By Louis C. Karpinski. With 4 plates showing pages of manuscripts in facsimile, and 25 diagrams in the text. Pp. vii + 164. $2.00.

Part II. The Prodromus of Nicolaus Steno's Latin Dissertation Concerning a Solid Body Enclosed by Process of Nature within a Solid. Translated into English by John G. Winter, with a Foreword by Professor William H. Hobbs. With 7 plates. Pp. vii + 169–283. $1.30.

Vol. XII. Studies in East Christian and Roman Art. By Charles R. Morey and Walter Dennison. (*Out of print.*)

Orders should be addressed to The Librarian, University of Michigan, Ann Arbor, Michigan.

Parts Sold Separately:

Part I. EAST CHRISTIAN PAINTINGS IN THE FREER COLLECTION. By Charles R. Morey. (*Out of print.*)

Part II. A GOLD TREASURE OF THE LATE ROMAN PERIOD. By Walter Dennison. With 54 plates, and 57 illustrations in the text. (*Out of print.*)

VOL. XIII. FRAGMENTS FROM THE CAIRO GENIZAH IN THE FREER COLLECTION. By Richard Gottheil and William H. Worrell. Text, with Translation and an Introduction. With 52 plates showing the different styles of writing in facsimile. Pp. xxxi + 273. Bound in cloth. $4.00.

VOL. XIV. TWO STUDIES IN LATER ROMAN AND BYZANTINE ADMINISTRATION. By A. E. R. Boak and James E. Dunlap. Pp. x + 324. Bound in cloth. $2.25.

Parts Sold Separately in Paper Covers:

Part I. THE MASTER OF THE OFFICES IN THE LATER ROMAN AND BYZANTINE EMPIRES. By Arthur E. R. Boak. (*Out of print.*)

Part II. THE OFFICE OF THE GRAND CHAMBERLAIN IN THE LATER ROMAN AND BYZANTINE EMPIRES. By James E. Dunlap. Pp. 164–324. $1.00.

VOL. XV. GREEK THEMES IN MODERN MUSICAL SETTINGS. By Albert A. Stanley. (*Out of print.*)

Parts Sold Separately in Paper Covers:

Part I. INCIDENTAL MUSIC TO PERCY MACKAYE'S DRAMA OF SAPPHO AND PHAON. Pp. 1–68. $0.90.

Part II. MUSIC TO THE ALCESTIS OF EURIPIDES WITH ENGLISH TEXT. Pp. 71–120. $0.80.

Part III. MUSIC FOR THE IPHIGENIA AMONG THE TAURIANS BY EURIPIDES WITH GREEK TEXT. Pp. 123–214. $0.75.

Part IV. TWO FRAGMENTS OF ANCIENT GREEK MUSIC. Pp. 217–225. $0.30.

Part V. MUSIC TO CANTICA OF THE MENAECHMI OF PLAUTUS. Pp. 229–263. $0.60.

Part VI. ATTIS: A SYMPHONIC POEM. Pp. 265–384. $1.00.

VOL. XVI. NICOMACHUS OF GERASA: INTRODUCTION TO ARITHMETIC. Translated into English by Martin Luther D'Ooge, with Studies in Greek Arithmetic by Frank Egleston Robbins and Louis C. Karpinski. (*Out of print.*)

VOLS. XVII–XX. ROYAL CORRESPONDENCE OF THE ASSYRIAN EMPIRE. Translated into English, with a transliteration of the text and a Commentary. By Leroy Waterman.

VOL. XVII. TRANSLATION AND TRANSLITERATION. Pp. x + 490. $4.50.

VOL. XVIII. TRANSLATION AND TRANSLITERATION. Pp. iv + 524. $4.50.

VOL. XIX. COMMENTARY. Pp. x + 377. $4.00.

VOL. XX. SUPPLEMENT AND INDEXES. (*In preparation.*)

Orders should be addressed to The Librarian, University of Michigan,
Ann Arbor, Michigan.

Vol. XXI. The Minor Prophets in the Freer Collection and the Berlin Fragment of Genesis. By Henry A. Sanders and Carl Schmidt. With 7 plates. Pp. xiii + 436. $3.50.

Vol. XXII. A Papyrus Codex of the Shepherd of Hermas, Together with a Fragment of the Mandates. By Campbell Bonner. With 5 plates. Pp. x + 137. $3.00.

Vol. XXIII. The Complete Commentary of Oecumenius on the Apocalypse: Now printed for the first time from Manuscripts at Messina, Rome, Salonika and Athos. By H. C. Hoskier. Pp. viii + 260. $4.00.

Vol. XXIV. Zenon Papyri in the University of Michigan Collection (= Michigan Papyri, Vol. I). By C. C. Edgar. Pp. xiv + 211. With 6 plates. $3.50.

Vol. XXV. Karanis: Topographical and Architectural Report of Excavations during the Seasons 1924–28. By A. E. R. Boak and E. Peterson. Pp. viii + 69. With 42 plates, 19 plans, and 1 map. $2.00.

Vol. XXVI. Coptic Sounds. By William H. Worrell, with an Appendix by Hide Shohara. Pp. xviii + 186. $2.50.

Vol. XXVII. Athenian Financial Documents of the Fifth Century. By B. D. Meritt. Pp. xiv. + 192 $3.50.

Vols. XXVIII–XXIX (= Michigan Papyri, Vols. II–III). Papyri from Tebtunis. By A. E. R. Boak.
Vol. XXVIII (= Michigan Papyri, Vol. II). Pp. xvi + 259. $3.50.
Vol. XXIX. (*In preparation.*)

Vol. XXX. Karanis: The Temples, Coin Hoards, Botanical and Zoölogical Reports, Seasons 1924–31. Edited by A. E. R. Boak. Pp. xii + 93. With 37 plates, 16 plans, and 4 diagrams. $2.50.

Vol. XXXI. Ancient Textiles from Egypt in the University of Michigan Collection. By Lillian M. Wilson. Pp. x + 77. With 23 plates. $2.50.

Vol. XXXII. Parthian Pottery from Seleucia on the Tigris. By Neilson C. Debevoise. Pp. xiv + 132. With 14 plates. $3.00.

Vol. XXXIII. The Athenian Assessment of 425 B.C. By B.D. Meritt and A. B. West. Pp. xiv + 112. With 2 plates and 17 figures. $2.50.

FACSIMILES OF MANUSCRIPTS
Size, 40.5 × 35 cm.

Facsimile of the Washington Manuscript of Deuteronomy and Joshua in the Freer Collection. With an Introduction by Henry A. Sanders. Pp. x; 201 heliotype plates.

Limited edition, distributed only to libraries, under certain conditions. A list of libraries containing this Facsimile is printed in *University of Michigan Studies, Humanistic Series,* Volume VIII, pp. 351–353.

Orders should be addressed to The Librarian, University of Michigan,
Ann Arbor, Michigan.

Size, 34 × 26 cm.

FACSIMILE OF THE WASHINGTON MANUSCRIPT OF THE FOUR GOSPELS IN THE FREER COLLECTION. With an Introduction by Henry A. Sanders. Pp. x; 372 heliotype plates and 2 colored plates.

Limited edition, distributed only to libraries, under certain conditions. A list of libraries containing this Facsimile is printed in *University of Michigan Studies, Humanistic Series*, Volume IX, pp. 317–320.

Size, 30.5 × 40.6 cm.

FACSIMILE OF THE WASHINGTON MANUSCRIPT OF THE MINOR PROPHETS IN THE FREER COLLECTION AND THE BERLIN FRAGMENT OF GENESIS. With an Introduction by Henry A. Sanders. With 130 plates.

Limited edition, distributed only to libraries, under certain conditions. A list of libraries containing this Facsimile is printed in *University of Michigan Studies, Humanistic Series*, Volume XXI, pp. 431–434.

THE JEROME LECTURES

LIFE AND LETTERS IN THE PAPYRI. By J. G. Winter. Pp. viii + 308. $3.50.

SCIENTIFIC SERIES

Size, 28 × 18.5 cm. 4°. Bound in Cloth.

VOL. I. THE CIRCULATION AND SLEEP. By John F. Shepard. Pp. ix + 83, with an Atlas of 63 plates, bound separately. Text and Atlas, $2.50.

VOL. II. STUDIES ON DIVERGENT SERIES AND SUMMABILITY. By Walter B. Ford. Pp. xi + 194. $2.50.

Size, 16 × 23.6 cm.

VOL. III. THE GEOLOGY OF THE NETHERLANDS EAST INDIES. By H. A. Brouwer. With 18 plates and 17 text figures. Pp. xii + 160. $3.00.

VOL. IV. THE GLACIAL ANTICYCLONES: THE POLES OF THE ATMOSPHERIC CIRCULATION. By William Herbert Hobbs. With 3 plates and 53 figures. Pp. xxiv + 198. $2.75.

VOLS. V–VIII. REPORTS OF THE GREENLAND EXPEDITIONS OF THE UNIVERSITY OF MICHIGAN (1926–31). W. H. Hobbs, Director.

VOL. V. Aërology, Expeditions of 1926 and 1927–29. With 23 plates and 30 text figures. Pp. x + 262. $6.00.

VOL. VI. Aërology, Expeditions of 1930–31. (*In preparation.*)

VOL. VII. Meteorology. (*In preparation.*)

VOL. VIII. Geology, Glaciology, Botany, etc. (*In preparation.*)

VOL. IX. THE GENUS DIAPORTHE NITSCHKE AND ITS SEGREGATES. By Lewis E. Wehmeyer. Pp. x + 335. With 18 Plates. $3.50.

VOL. X. THE DISTRIBUTION OF THE CURRENTS OF ACTION AND OF INJURY DISPLAYED BY HEART MUSCLE AND OTHER EXCITABLE TISSUES. By F. N. Wilson, A. G. Macleod, and P. S. Barker. Pp. viii + 59. $1.50.

Orders should be addressed to The Librarian, University of Michigan, Ann Arbor, Michigan.

MEMOIRS OF THE UNIVERSITY OF MICHIGAN MUSEUMS

Size, 26 × 17 cm. 4°. Bound in Cloth.

Vol. I. The Whip Snakes and Racers: Genera Masticophis and Coluber. By A. I. Ortenburger, University of Oklahoma. With 36 plates and 64 text figures. Pp. xviii + 247. $6.00.

Vol. II. Description of the Skull of a New Form of Phytosaur, with Notes on the Characters of Described North American Phytosaurs. By E. C. Case, University of Michigan. With 7 plates and 24 text figures. Pp. vi + 56. $2.00.

UNIVERSITY OF MICHIGAN PUBLICATIONS

General Editor: EUGENE S. McCARTNEY

HUMANISTIC PAPERS

Size, 22.7 × 15.2 cm. 8°. Bound in Cloth.

The Life and Work of George Sylvester Morris. A Chapter in the History of American Thought in the Nineteenth Century. By Robert M. Wenley. Pp. xv + 332. $1.50.

Henry Philip Tappan: Philosopher and University President. By Charles Perry. Pp. xii + 475. $3.25.

Latin and Greek in American Education, with Symposia on the Value of Humanistic Studies, Revised Edition. Edited by Francis W. Kelsey. Pp. xiii + 360. $2.00.

The Menaechmi of Plautus. The Latin Text, with a Translation by Joseph H. Drake, University of Michigan. Pp. xi + 130. Paper covers. $0.60.

LANGUAGE AND LITERATURE

Vol. I. Studies in Shakespeare, Milton and Donne. By Members of the English Department of the University of Michigan. Pp. viii + 232. $2.50.

Vol. II. Elizabethan Proverb Lore in Lyly's 'Euphues' and in Pettie's 'Petite Pallace,' with Parallels from Shakespeare. By Morris P. Tilley. Pp. x + 461. $3.50.

Vol. III. The Social Mode of Restoration Comedy. By Kathleen M. Lynch. Pp. x + 242. $2.50.

Vol. IV. Stuart Politics in Chapman's 'Tragedy of Chabot.' By Norma D. Solve. Pp. x + 176. $2.50.

Vol. V. El Libro del Cauallero Zifar: Part I, Text. By C. P. Wagner Pp. xviii + 532, with 9 plates. $5.00.

Vol. VI. El Libro del Cauallero Zifar: Part II, Commentary. By C. P. Wagner. (*In preparation.*)

Orders should be addressed to The Librarian, University of Michigan, Ann Arbor, Michigan.

Vol. VII. Strindberg's Dramatic Expressionism. By C. E. W. L. Dahlström. Pp. xii + 242. $2.50.

Vol. VIII. Essays and Studies in English and Comparative Literature. By Members of the English Department of the University of Michigan. Pp. viii + 231. $2.50.

Vol. IX. Toward the Understanding of Shelley. By Bennett Weaver, University of Michigan. Pp. xii + 258. $2.50.

Vol. X. Essays and Studies in English and Comparative Literature. By Members of the English Department of the University of Michigan. Pp. vi + 278. $2.50.

Vol. XI. French Modal Syntax in the Sixteenth Century. By Newton S. Bement. Pp. xviii + 168. $2.50.

Vol. XII. The Intellectual Milieu of John Dryden. By Louis I. Bredvold. Pp. viii + 189. $2.50.

Three Centuries of French Poetic Theory (1328-1630). By W. F. Patterson. (*In press.*)

HISTORY AND POLITICAL SCIENCE

(*The first three volumes of this series were published as "Historical Studies," under the direction of the Department of History. Volumes IV and V were published without numbers.*)

Vol. I. A History of the President's Cabinet. By Mary Louise Hinsdale. (*Out of print.*)

Vol. II. English Rule in Gascony, 1199–1259, with Special Reference to the Towns. By Frank Burr Marsh. Pp. xi + 178. $1.25.

Vol. III. The Color Line in Ohio: A History of Race Prejudice in a Typical Northern State. By Frank Uriah Quillan. (*Out of print.*)

Vol. IV. The Senate and Treaties, 1789–1817. The Development of the Treaty-Making Functions of the United States Senate during Their Formative Period. By Ralston Hayden. Pp. xvi + 237. $1.50.

Vol. V. William Plumer's Memorandum of Proceedings in the United States Senate, 1803–1807. Edited by Everett Somerville Brown. Pp. xi + 673. $3.50.

Vol. VI. The Grain Supply of England during the Napoleonic Period. By W. F. Galpin. Pp. xi + 305. $3.00.

Vol. VII. Eighteenth Century Documents Relating to the Royal Forests, the Sheriffs and Smuggling: Selected from the Shelburne Manuscripts in the William L. Clements Library. By Arthur Lyon Cross. With 4 plates. Pp. xviii + 328. $3.00.

Orders should be addressed to The Librarian, University of Michigan, Ann Arbor, Michigan.

Vol. VIII. The Low Countries and the Hundred Years' War, 1326–1347. By Henry S. Lucas. Pp. xviii + 696. $4.00.

Vol. IX. The Anglo-French Treaty of Commerce of 1860 and the Progress of the Industrial Revolution in France. By A. L. Dunham. Pp. xiv + 409. $3.00.

Vol. X. The Youth of Erasmus. By A. Hyma. Pp. xii + 350. With 8 plates and 2 maps. $3.00.

CONTRIBUTIONS FROM THE MUSEUM OF PALEONTOLOGY

(*A list of the separate papers in Volumes II–IV will be sent upon request.*)

Vol. I. The Stratigraphy and Fauna of the Hackberry Stage of the Upper Devonian, By Carroll Lane Fenton and Mildred Adams Fenton. With 45 plates, 9 text figures, and 1 map. Pp. xi + 260. $2.75.

Vol. II. Consisting of 14 papers. With 41 plates, 38 text figures, and 1 map. Pp. ix + 240. $3.00.

Vol. III. Consisting of 13 papers. With 64 plates, 49 text figures, and 1 map. Pp. viii + 275. $3.50.

Vol. IV. Consisting of miscellaneous papers. (*In progress.*)

ARCHAEOLOGICAL REPORTS

Preliminary Report upon the Excavations at Tel Umar, Iraq, Conducted by the University of Michigan and the Toledo Museum of Art. Leroy Waterman, Director. With 13 plates and 7 text figures. Pp. x + 62. $1.50. Bound in paper.

Second Preliminary Report upon the Excavations at Tel Umar, Iraq, Conducted by the University of Michigan, the Toledo Museum of Art, and the Cleveland Museum of Art. Leroy Waterman, Director. With 26 plates and 12 text figures. Pp. xii + 78. $1.50. Bound in paper.

PAPERS OF THE MICHIGAN ACADEMY OF SCIENCE, ARTS AND LETTERS

(Containing Papers submitted at Annual Meetings)

Editors: EUGENE S. McCARTNEY AND PETER OKKELBERG

Size, 24.2 × 16.5 cm. 8°. Bound in Cloth.

Vol. I (1921). Pp. xi + 424. $2.00.

Vol. II (1922). Pp. xi + 226. $2.00. Bound in paper, $1.50.

Vol. III (1923). Pp. xii + 473. $3.00. Bound in paper, $2.25.

Vol. IV (1924), Part I. Pp. xii + 631. $3.00. Bound in paper, $2.25.

Orders should be addressed to The Librarian, University of Michigan,
Ann Arbor, Michigan.

Vol. IV (1924), Part II. A Key to the Snakes of the United States, Canada and Lower California. By Frank N. Blanchard. Pp. xiii + 65. Cloth. $1.75.

Vol. V (1925). Pp. xii + 479. $3.00. Bound in paper, $2.25.

Vol. VI (1926). (Papers in botany only.) Pp. xii + 406. $3.00. Bound in paper, $2.25.

Vol. VII (1926). (No papers in botany.) Pp. xii + 435. $3.00. Bound in paper, $2.25.

Vol. VIII (1927). Pp. xiv + 456. $3.00. Bound in paper, $2.25.

Vol. IX (1928). (Papers in botany and forestry only.) Pp. xiv + 597. $4.00. Bound in paper, $2.25.

Vol. X (1928). (No papers in botany or forestry.) Pp. xvii + 620. $4.00. Bound in paper, $2.25.

Vol. XI (1929). (Papers in botany and zoölogy only.) Pp. xii + 494. $3.50. Bound in paper, $2.25.

Vol. XII (1929). (No papers in botany or zoölogy.) Pp. xii + 348. $3.00. Bound in paper, $2.25.

Vol. XIII (1930). (Papers in botany and zoölogy only.) Pp. xii + 603. $4.00. Bound in paper, $2.25.

Vol. XIV (1930). (No papers in botany or zoölogy.) Pp. xv + 650. $4.00. Bound in paper, $2.25.

Vol. XV (1931). (Papers in botany, forestry, and zoölogy only.) Pp. x + 511. $3.50. Bound in paper, $2.25.

Vol. XVI (1931). (No papers in botany, forestry, or zoölogy.)..Pp. x + 521. $3.50. Bound in paper, $2.25.

Vol. XVII (1932). (Papers in botany, forestry, and zoölogy only.) Pp. x + 738. $4.00. Bound in paper, $2.25.

Vol. XVIII (1932). (No papers in botany, forestry, or zoölogy.) Pp. xiv + 623. $4.00. Bound in paper, $2.25.

Vol. XIX (1933). Pp. xii + 662. $4.00. Bound in paper, $2.25.

*Orders should be addressed to The Librarian, University of Michigan,
Ann Arbor, Michigan.*